Advance Acclaim for
What You Must Think of Me

"With warmth, candor and insight, this highly gifted young writer shares her personal struggle with a serious yet treatable disorder that is often misdiagnosed and grossly misunderstood. Emily takes the reader along on her courageous journey toward recovery, while offering solid information, help and hope to individuals suffering from social anxiety disorder, as well as to family members and friends who want to help."

—Jerilyn Ross, M.A., LIC.S.W., Director,
The Ross Center for Anxiety & Related Disorders,
Washington, DC, and author of Triumph Over Fear

"Ford bravely offers an accurate account of the frustrations of social anxiety disorder, and the paths to treatment, including how to navigate the difficulties of the mental health system, how to identify an expert in SAD, and how to make the most of the therapeutic experience. This will be an excellent resource for adolescents, young adults, and their parents."

—Dean McKay, Ph.D., A.B.P.P.,
Department of Psychology, Fordham University

"For anyone who has shouldered the enormous burden of social anxiety disorder, *What You Must Think of Me* will be a valuable resource. Emily Ford gives her readers a rare glimpse into the tortured world of a young person struggling with SAD—the isolation, the depression, and her eventual triumph over this devastating illness. Her story is one of hope, humor, and an incredible will to survive, and will both inspire and educate readers who will recognize their own struggles within these pages."

—Jamie Blyth, author of Fear is No Longer My Reality:
How I Overcame Panic and Social
Anxiety Disorder—and You Can Too

THE ANNENBERG FOUNDATION TRUST AT SUNNYLANDS

The Annenberg Foundation Trust at Sunnylands' Adolescent Mental Health Initiative

Patrick E. Jamieson, Ph.D., *series editor*

In addition to *What You Must Think of Me*, other books in this series for young people are planned on the following topics:

Bipolar Disorder (2006)—now available:
Mind Race: A Firsthand Account of One Teenager's Experience With Bipolar Disorder,
by Patrick E. Jamieson, Ph.D., with Moira A. Rynn, M.D.

Depression (2007)—now available:
Monochrome Days: A Firsthand Account of One Teenager's Experience With Depression,
by Cait Irwin, with Dwight L. Evans, M.D., and Linda Wasmer Andrews

Eating Disorders (2007)
Next to Nothing: A Firsthand Account of One Teenager's Experience With an Eating Disorder,
by Carrie Arnold, with B. Timothy Walsh, M.D.

Schizophrenia (2007)
Me, Myself, and Them: A Firsthand Account of One Young Person's Experience With Schizophrenia,
by Kurt Snyder, with Raquel E. Gur, M.D., Ph.D., and Linda Wasmer Andrews

Obsessive-Compulsive Disorder (2008)
The Thought that Counts: A Firsthand Account of One Teenager's Experience with Obsessive-Compulsive Disorder, by Jared Douglas Kant, with Martin Franklin, Ph.D., and Linda Wasmer Andrews

Substance Abuse (2008)
Chasing the High: A Firsthand Account of One Young Person's Experience with Substance Abuse, by Kyle Keegan, with Howard B. Moss, M.D., and Beryl Lieff Benderly

Suicide Prevention (2008)
Eight Stories Up: An Adolescent Chooses Hope Over Suicide, by DeQuincy A. Lezine, Ph.D., with David Brent, M.D.

Also available in the series for parents and other adults:

If Your Adolescent Has Depression or Bipolar Disorder (2005)
Dwight L. Evans, M.D., and Linda Wasmer Andrews

If Your Adolescent Has an Eating Disorder (2005)
B. Timothy Walsh, M.D., and V. L. Cameron

If Your Adolescent Has an Anxiety Disorder (2006)
Edna B. Foa, Ph.D., and Linda Wasmer Andrews

If Your Adolescent Has Schizophrenia (2006)
Raquel E. Gur, M.D., Ph.D., and Ann Braden Johnson, Ph.D.

What You Must Think of Me

A Firsthand Account of One Teenager's Experience With Social Anxiety Disorder

Emily Ford

with Michael R. Liebowitz, M.D., and Linda Wasmer Andrews

The Annenberg Foundation Trust at Sunnylands'
Adolescent Mental Health Initiative

THE ANNENBERG
PUBLIC POLICY CENTER
OF THE UNIVERSITY OF PENNSYLVANIA

OXFORD
UNIVERSITY PRESS

2007

OXFORD
UNIVERSITY PRESS

Oxford University Press, Inc., publishes works that further
Oxford University's objective of excellence
in research, scholarship, and education.

The Annenberg Foundation Trust at Sunnylands
The Annenberg Public Policy Center of the University of Pennsylvania
Oxford University Press

Oxford   New York
Auckland   Cape Town   Dar es Salaam   Hong Kong   Karachi
Kuala Lumpur   Madrid   Melbourne   Mexico City   Nairobi
New Delhi   Shanghai   Taipei   Toronto

With offices in
Argentina   Austria   Brazil   Chile   Czech Republic   France   Greece
Guatemala   Hungary   Italy   Japan   Poland   Portugal   Singapore
South Korea   Switzerland   Thailand   Turkey   Ukraine   Vietnam

Library of Congress Cataloging-in-Publication Data
Ford, Emily, 1979–
What you must think of me: a firsthand account of one teenager's
experience with social anxiety disorder / by Emily Ford with Michael
R. Liebowitz and Linda Wasmer Andrews.
    p. cm.—(Adolescent mental health initiative)
Includes bibliographical references and index.
ISBN 978-0-19-531302-4; 978-0-19-531303-1 (pbk)
1. Social phobia in adolescence—Popular works.   I. Liebowitz,
Michael R.   II. Andrews, Linda Wasmer.   III. Title.
RJ506.S63F67 2007
616.85'22500835—dc22   2006102285

Printed in the United States of America
on acid-free paper

To Dr. "Q.", to whom I owe a world of gratitude,
and to J. R. and everyone at T.R.C. who changes lives

Contents

Three
Not Just Another Shy Teenager   25

Four
First Steps Toward Recovery   37

Five
A Long Road Filled With Potholes   52

Six
Five Days That Changed My Life   73

Foreword

The Adolescent Mental Health Initiative (AMHI) was created by The Annenberg Foundation Trust at Sunnylands to share with mental health professionals, parents, and adolescents the advances in treatment and prevention now available to adolescents with mental health disorders. The Initiative was made possible by the generosity and vision of Ambassadors Walter and Leonore Annenberg, and the project was administered through the Annenberg Public Policy Center of the University of Pennsylvania in partnership with Oxford University Press.

The Initiative began in 2003 with the convening, in Philadelphia and New York, of seven scholarly commissions made up of over 150 leading psychiatrists and psychologists from around the country. Chaired by Drs. Edna B. Foa, Dwight L. Evans, B. Timothy Walsh, Martin E. P. Seligman, Raquel E. Gur, Charles P. O'Brien, and Herbert Hendin, these commissions were tasked with assessing the state of scientific research on the prevalent mental disorders whose onset occurs predominantly between the ages of 10 and 22. Their collective

findings now appear in a book for mental health professionals and policy makers titled *Treating and Preventing
Adolescent Mental Health Disorders* (2005). As the first product
of the Initiative, that book also identified a research agenda
that would best advance our ability to prevent and treat these
disorders, among them anxiety disorders, depression and bipolar disorder, eating disorders, substance abuse, and schizophrenia.

The second prong of the Initiative's three-part effort is a
series of smaller books for general readers. Some of the books
are designed primarily for parents of adolescents with a specific
mental health disorder. And some, including this one, are
aimed at adolescents themselves who are struggling with a
mental illness. All of the books draw their scientific information in part from the AMHI professional volume, presenting it
in a manner that is accessible to general readers of different
ages. The "teen books" also feature the real-life story of one
young person who has struggled with—and now manages—
a given mental illness. They serve as both a source of solid
research about the illness and as a roadmap to recovery for
afflicted young people. Thus they offer a unique combination
of medical science and firsthand practical wisdom in an effort
to inspire adolescents to take an active role in their own recovery.

The third part of the Sunnylands Adolescent Mental
Health Initiative consists of two Web sites. The first, www.
CopeCareDeal.org, addresses teens. The second, www.oup.
com/us/teenmentalhealth, provides updates to the medical
community on matters discussed in *Treating and Preventing
Adolescent Mental Health Disorders*, the AMHI professional
book.

We hope that you find this volume, as one of the fruits of the Initiative, to be helpful and enlightening.

Patrick Jamieson, Ph.D.
Series Editor
Adolescent Risk Communication Institute
Annenberg Public Policy Center
University of Pennsylvania
Philadelphia, PA

Preface

"Just get over it." "You're making a mountain out of a molehill." "I was shy too at your age."

Sound familiar?

Like most people with social anxiety disorder, you've heard the dismissive comments before. You may have repeated them to yourself as your heart was racing, your breath shallow, your cheeks burning, and your head swimming with fear of humiliation. *People do this every day, so why can't I? It's not that big a deal, right?*

It *is* a big deal, and you deserve credit for having the courage to pick up a book on social anxiety disorder. Whether you're reading these pages in the very public aisle of a bookstore or in the privacy of your bedroom, simply by opening to this page, you've taken a giant leap toward conquering your fear. You no longer have to suffer the pain of social anxiety in isolation.

You are not alone. About 15 million Americans struggle with social anxiety disorder. That's more than the number of men, women, and children living in New York, Los Angeles, Houston, and Denver combined! So where are they? Like you, many are probably spending a great deal of time on their own, fading into the crowd, not drawing much attention to themselves. They're behind you at the supermarket, struggling to write a check at the clothing store, and nervously taking your order over the phone. They're sure you must be judging them. But what they don't know is that you're too consumed with your own worries to notice anyone else's.

More Than Ordinary Shyness

When I first began referring to myself as a person with social anxiety disorder, I feared people would believe I was putting on airs by giving shyness a dressed-up title. In a society consumed with syndromes, disorders, and pharmaceutical advertisements, I assumed it appeared as though I'd hopped on the "we're all disordered" bandwagon, hiding a personality flaw behind the more sophisticated and increasingly popular term *anxiety*. Still, *I* knew social anxiety disorder was a real condition substantially different from shyness. It had very real symptoms and very real consequences.

I wasn't sure millions of others truly suffered from social anxiety until I attended a meeting for people with the problem. I found myself in a room full of uncomfortable men and women explaining how they avoided telephone conversations, get-togethers, and situations that called for asserting themselves. They discussed how social anxiety hindered their lives, from their experiences at school and work to their personal relationships. Most agreed social anxiety had been present from an early age, and some claimed they'd suffered with it for as long as they could remember.

Over time, as I got to know some of the group members more intimately, I was shocked to discover that even my strangest, most private fears were not un-ique to me!

I hadn't wanted to go to that first meeting. Joining a close circle of ten people fidgeting nervously with pencils and

...I was shocked to discover that even my strangest, most private fears were not unique to me!

handouts wasn't something I particularly looked forward to doing. It was my therapist's suggestion, one that I'd avoided acting on for months. But in looking around the group, I didn't see the mismatched, floor-staring, shy misfits of TV lore. Instead, I saw the faces of lawyers, artists, secretaries, even politicians. I decided to give the group a shot—and that's what I ask you to do with this book as well.

The Faces Behind These Pages

My story of dealing with social anxiety disorder in school, its eventual effect on my well-being, and the steps I took to overcome it is recounted in the following pages. I am Emily, a 27-year-old who has battled social anxiety disorder since the fourth grade. Thanks to the loving support of my family and some very caring and talented experts, I am no longer a victim of the condition that imprisoned me for nearly two decades. My mornings, afternoons, and evenings aren't spent in lonely solitude. Though at one time I confined myself to a secluded cabin on 40 acres of woods, today I love the life that takes me out on the busy streets of Washington, DC, every day. I've found in myself a willingness to try things I never thought possible, and I no longer go to sleep dreading the day to come. A year and a half ago, I would have laughed in the face of anyone who told me a joyful, fearless life complete with friends who didn't think of me as crazy was possible, *but it is.*

I'm trained as a high school English teacher, not a psychiatrist. To ensure that the medical and scientific parts of the book are accurate, I have been lucky enough to team up with one of the nation's foremost experts on social anxiety disorder. Dr. Michael R. Liebowitz is a professor of clinical psychiatry at the College of Physicians and Surgeons of Columbia University Medical Center in New York. From 1982 to 2006, he was also director of the Anxiety Disorders Clinic at the New York State Psychiatric Institute. In 2003, Dr. Liebowitz was a member of a distinguished professional commission on adolescent anxiety disorders. The commission was convened by the Annenberg Foundation Trust at Sunnylands, a nonprofit group that aims to enhance mental health among young people. This book is, in part, an outgrowth of a report issued by that commission.

Social anxiety disorder has only recently begun to get the scientific respect it deserves. Dr. Liebowitz has been instrumental in bringing attention to this long-neglected disorder. Among other things, he developed a widely used assessment tool for adults called the Liebowitz Social Anxiety Scale, which has since been adapted for children and adolescents. His scale was used as the major outcome measure in studies that looked at the use of medication to treat social anxiety disorder in people under age 18. In addition, Dr. Liebowitz chaired an American Psychiatric Association work group that established the standard diagnostic criteria for the various types of anxiety disorders.

The third member of our writing team is Linda Wasmer Andrews, a journalist who has specialized in mental health issues for more than two decades. Together, my coauthors and I have written a book that looks at social anxiety disorder from every angle. It's my story, but it's your story, too. We've tried to answer the questions that real teenagers and young adults often ask, and we've provided practical tips on coping with social anxiety at home and school.

What's Special About This Book

Information about social anxiety is everywhere today. It's broadcast on television talk shows, printed in magazine articles, and found only clicks away on the Internet. I asked myself, why add another person's story to the mix? The truth is, I find that many books about social anxiety disorder cover only the prettier aspects of the condition. Many selectively disregard its less discussed, more painful, even embarrassing side. Yet the problem runs deeper than the racing heart, gurgling stomach, shortness of breath, and avoidance of social interaction. Social anxiety has everything to do with extreme self-doubt, insecurity, and even a dislike of oneself that doesn't go away when social triggers are out of the picture. It's no wonder that many people with social anxiety disorder also sufferer from depression. Frankly, it's a sad and lonely place to be.

But there's hope! My second aim in writing the book is to prove, actually *prove*, that many of a socially anxious person's perceptions are misconstrued. I spent each day of high school believing deep down that my teachers hated me. I thought that at every moment people were making fun of me and whispering nasty comments underneath their breath. I feared one day I would completely lose control, say or do something off the wall, and inevitably end up in a mental institution. As I was preparing to write this book, I was determined to put those painful perceptions to the reality test, but how?

One day, it came to me: I would return to my old school, interview my old classmates and teachers, and record what they actually recalled thinking about me—the good, the bad, and the ugly. A few months later, there I was—the person who had once been paralyzed with fear able to conquer anxiety enough to return and face those who had terrified me the most. In these pages, you'll be able to compare my previous assumptions alongside the actual thoughts of my classmates and teachers. It was a journey of self-discovery that changed my life.

Fighting the Battle Together

If you're struggling with social anxiety, I strongly encourage you to seek help as early as you can, whether it's now, once you're 50 pages into this book, or after you've turned the final page. This is easier said than done, I know. But as you read on, I'll offer suggestions on where to turn and how to take those difficult first steps. Consider me your advocate, a fellow sufferer who knows not only how hard it is to fight this disorder, but also how rewarding the effort ultimately can be.

Like so many others with similar stories, I hear myself saying that I wish I had sought help as soon as I recognized something was wrong. It would have saved years of struggle, depression, and isolation. These are not scars I wear proudly; they're the result of fearing what someone might think if I were to speak up and ask for help. *The bravest thing I've ever done* was to reach out and actively seek the assistance I desperately wanted and knew that I needed. I made

> *The bravest thing I've ever done was to reach out and actively seek the assistance I desperately wanted and knew that I needed.*

that step for no one but me, and it has made all the difference in my life.

I encourage you to do the same. It won't be easy by any stretch of the word, but it will be worth it. There are wonderful, caring people ready and willing to help. A happier life is waiting.

What You Must Think of Me

Chapter One

Self-Conscious to the Nth Degree

There was a time I would have been up nights preparing my script and reciting it to an outfit (complete down to its underwear) hung weeks in advance behind the bedroom door. Every worst-case scenario would have been thought through, and I'd have prepared a litany of excuses in the event I froze, stared off into space, or filled with tears. But nine-hours-and-counting to a day that could prove most embarrassing, I was drifting in and out of sleep thousands of feet over a storm system in New Jersey. A girl who had for years traveled exclusively by Greyhound was flying, *actually flying*, from Washington, DC, to northern New York without keeping a white-knuckle grip on the armrest or reworking the opening lines to the next day's meetings in her head.

I was headed back to the town where I had grown up to find out what type of impression I had *really* made on former classmates, teachers, and neighbors. Had they, in fact, seen me the way I had once seen myself: awkward, always trying too hard, and more than a little unstable? I would be interviewing people from my past to find out. It was research for this book,

1

but it was also a chance to learn more about myself as I revisited the place where my social anxiety disorder had taken root.

The weekend could set my progress back for months if my confidence was shaken by sideways glances and forced smiles, clear indicators I had really lost it this time. Rumors about me dropping out of college, quitting two teaching jobs, and living in a cabin on the outskirts of town had circulated among my old friends and neighbors. Now the girl was back to make another spectacle of herself? Hadn't she embarrassed herself enough, or was she so far gone that she no longer knew when to lie low and admit she didn't have all of her wits about her?

It was possible they'd think I was crazy, but I was going back.

What Social Anxiety Is All About

Even in high school, part of me knew that I was not at the center of everyone's universe. I didn't believe that my classmates went to bed thinking about how I wasn't asked to slow dance on Friday night. I knew my teachers didn't discuss my poor spelling with their spouses at the dinner table. I did assume, however, that when I was among friends or teachers, my awkwardness was too obvious to ignore. I believed everyone around me was exchanging subtle signs and signals, conveying to one another that for any of a number of reasons, I was out of place. This is the very convincing yet irrational belief that lies at the heart of social anxiety disorder.

I believed everyone around me was exchanging subtle signs and signals, conveying to one another that for any of a number of reasons, I was out of place.

As its name implies, social anxiety disorder falls into the category of mental illnesses called anxiety disorders, all of which involve some type of excessive fear or worry that is recurrent or long-lasting. Of course, we all feel anxious or worried from time to time. But to qualify as a disorder, the symptoms must be disruptive enough to cause distress or interfere with day-to-day activities.

In social anxiety disorder, the fear centers around social situations that involve being in the presence of unfamiliar people or the possibility of scrutiny by others. In a nutshell, people with this disorder are preoccupied with the fear that

---

What's in a Name?

Everyone is a little socially anxious from time to time, but that doesn't mean everyone has social anxiety *disorder*. The following personality traits and behavior patterns can look similar to social anxiety disorder, at least on the surface. However, they're often just normal variations in the way people think, feel, and behave.

- Shyness—A general tendency to pull back from social situations.
- Introversion—A general tendency toward having a quiet, reserved nature.
- Behavioral inhibition—A pattern of timid, fearful behavior around strangers or new situations.
- Performance anxiety—Stress and worry about how you will perform on some activity that's done in front of others. Examples include stage fright, test anxiety, and pre-game jitters.

The key difference is that these traits and behaviors don't cause the same degree of difficulty or distress as social anxiety disorder. Many healthy individuals are shy or introverted, and many people with no anxiety disorder experience mild behavioral inhibition or occasional performance anxiety. It's only when distress or dysfunction enters the picture that the possibility of a disorder is considered.

they'll embarrass themselves or be held up to ridicule. While everyone feels self-conscious occasionally, for people with social anxiety, the fear can reach disabling proportions.

Whether standing at center stage or blending into a crowd, sufferers of social anxiety feel as if all eyes are on them. They know their fear is excessive or unreasonable, but they feel powerless to control it. As a result, they may endure social situations only with great discomfort, or they may spend considerable time and energy avoiding such situations. Eventually, the anxiety may consume more and more of their life, getting in the way of school, hobbies, work, and relationships.

For some, the extreme anxiety is limited to a few, specific situations. As an example, some people are petrified of public speaking. To make matters worse, they may fear that their red face and shaky voice will betray their distress to all around. Others dread eating or writing in public, and they may worry that their trembling hands will give them away. Still others become very anxious in one-on-one conversation, convinced that they'll inevitably be seen as boring and socially inept.

And then there are those like me, whose fears encompass a wide range of social situations, from going to school to attending parties, and from striking up a private conversation to traveling in a crowded plane. The term *generalized* is sometimes applied to this type of wide-ranging social anxiety. As a rule, it tends to start earlier and last longer than social anxiety that is confined to a specific situation.

Because it affects virtually every facet of life, generalized social anxiety can severely limit a person's activities, cutting that individual off from the rest of the world as if marooned on a personal desert island. Back in high school, I felt a general sense of anxiety about being around most other people, most of the time. I knew something was wrong, and I waited for someone to spot me and rescue me before I finally realized I had to take the first steps to help myself. It would be years before I finally sent up an SOS, and years after that before I was ready to revisit the place where socially anxiety began interfering with my life.

My Journey to Self-Discovery

The school required visitors to announce themselves at the office and wear a conspicuous three-by-five yellow sticker. This would have been laughable back when I was a student, when an unfamiliar face stood out more than if the word VISITOR had been tattooed across the poor stranger's forehead. Times had changed. The building had been modernized with thick doors, new Plexiglas barriers, and walls where none had stood before. A new generation of teachers had replaced many of the names that were staples from my school days.

I headed down the hall feeling only a little nervous, without the feigned pretentiousness that I had once worn like armor. Years ago, I would have lifted my head, pursed my lips, and walked with a heavy step in an attempt to hide the fact that my insides had turned to jelly. But this day was different. I was prepared to bump into anyone, including my former health teacher. He warmly extended his hand, asked what I was up to, and wished me luck. I didn't freeze. I didn't recite practiced lines or dwell on his demeanor. For once in my life, I was comfortable in who I was at that moment.

My biggest fear about revisiting my old school was not that I might be told that I had once been considered antisocial and unlikable. Rather, I feared everyone telling me in dull, generic terms that I had been a hard-working, quiet student, musically inclined with some very creative ideas. I was concerned that platitudes such as these were what teachers believed I'd come back to school to hear, and that they'd rather say nice things than relate that I had been an awkward, immature, attention-hungry girl who wrote strangely themed essays with too many adjectives. I had come to believe that many from my past thought of me as arrogant, always digging up underhanded ways to draw attention to myself. Now here I was again, a little concerned that others might view my return as just another ploy to get them to say that I was good, sweet, and talented, and that poor me was more than shy—I was *socially anxious*.

That was the fear, but it was one that I was prepared to face. No longer was I a shell that needed to be filled with other people's kind words. I thought back on the phrase taught to me a year ago: I am not responsible for other people's actions or behavior. I had come a long way from the girl who had once been so desperate for everyone's approval, yet so convinced she could never attain it.

I am not responsible for other people's actions or behavior.

What My Teachers Remembered

I prepared myself for reluctant, awkward exchanges. I was welcomed with more eagerness to help than I could have dreamed of receiving.

When I knocked on the door of my former French teacher, she greeted me warmly, asked about my family, and showed me pictures of hers. Then I told her about the project I was working on, and I didn't detect any hesitancy or funny looks.

"Do you know what I remember about you?" she asked.

I shrank in my chair. "When I cried on the oral part of the French Regents Exam?" Ten years ago, I never would have had the courage to give such an honest answer.

She laughingly waved off my words. "That? Oh, no. Students cry all of the time."

I was sure I was remembered for crying on that test. And what about the times I nervously stuttered through answers, or the embarrassing stories I put in a report on my family history? What about the horrible burnt peanut butter cookies I made for her because she gave me a ride to a meeting, or the time she went out of her way so that selfish me could go to Shakespeare and Company on our French club trip? What about my nervous way of filling crepes during the annual Mardi Gras festival, or all of the times I'd come into her room a nervous wreck because her class followed my driving days in drivers' education? According to her, I was like a lot of other students:

> As I think back to when Emily was one of my students, she was so much like many other young women who are uncomfortable in their own skin as they are still finding out who they really are.
>
> —Mrs. W.

In subsequent interviews with other teachers, Mrs. H. didn't even recall at first that I had taken chemistry, one of my most challenging courses from one of the teachers who intimidated me most. Mrs. R. didn't mention the competitive and stubborn way I'd acted in chorus and how I vied for parts in musicals. An old classmate, who was now teaching art at the school and who I feared would give any excuse not to see me, asked all about my family and cheerily filled me in on what she and some of our other classmates were up to. And yet, these were the people I had feared for years, thinking their only recollections of me were as an annoying girl who would never be capable of redeeming herself.

But what really made the experience of going back one of the most rewarding of my life was that it was something deeply personal, something no one else could have suggested I do. This was *my* journey. Confronting the harsh memories of my teenage years meant bolstering my courage to take action instead of letting bad feelings linger on. Ten years had passed, and I no longer wanted to cringe at any reference to my old school or dread the possibility of bumping into someone associated with it. I no longer wanted to run from the fear—and I look with pride on what I can say without exaggeration was a pivotal journey.

Conversations With My Past

The premise of meeting to discuss social anxiety disorder apparently did not seem awkward to anyone. In fact, the more candor that was brought to the subject, the more others shared stories about their own private battles. I was stunned and delighted that I was not only received so warmly, but that I was entrusted with some very personal stories. I felt human. I felt accepted.

On Sunday evening, I walked to the home of an old friend's family—a family I hadn't dropped in on in 15 years. Despite the fact that I had interrupted dinner complete with candlelight, cake, and relatives, I was welcomed with open arms. Not one member of the family made me feel as though I was, or ever had been, crazy.

They showed me pictures. They laughed over memories. My old friend's younger sister sat me down in the living room and engaged me in conversation on everything from graduate studies to boyfriends to trips abroad. She talked about how so many things change, and how wonderful it is to find a sense of belonging among friends. In three hours, I had vanquished the fear of running into my neighbors on the street, and in the process, I had made a new friend.

Not every reception was as warm, which in its own way was a blessing. When I was a senior in high school, one of my teachers told me we "didn't gel" that year. It was true. The tension between us was palpable for reasons that were hard to define. Although this teacher was friendly when I finally worked up the courage to see her a half hour before my trip was to draw to a close, our brief meeting felt artificially upbeat. Part of me wanted to wipe the slate clean and apologize for our uncomfortable history, but part of me knew that might not be realistic. Some people simply don't hit it off as readily as others.

I could have replayed that meeting in my head for weeks, allowing it to devalue the earlier days of my visit, but I didn't. For much of the plane ride home, I thought about it, yes. I wondered whether there was something I might have done better, but then I let it go. Not all challenges are met with an easy fix. The exchange was beneficial because it helped me stay grounded in reality, which isn't always picture perfect. My journey had been overwhelmingly positive, but it wasn't a fairy tale. As it turned out, some of my misgivings about this particular meeting were justified, but after all was said and done, I'd lived through it.

The Danger of Doing Nothing

I'm among the lucky ones, because I eventually sought and received the help I needed. With proper treatment, it's possible to have a rich, rewarding, socially active life. My anxiety is unlikely to

With proper treatment, it's possible to have a rich, rewarding, socially active life.

ever disappear completely, especially in times of stress. But now I'm prepared with strategies for handling it, and I know where to turn when extra help is required. Without treatment, though, social anxiety disorder can lead to serious problems at school and later at work. Just as importantly, it can sap much of the enjoyment from life.

Many adults trivialize the torture each school day brings to so many. It's hard for some to recognize that a teenager can suffer from disabling social anxiety that is much more substantial than an occasional bout of test anxiety or a tongue-tied

---

A Brief History of Social Anxiety Disorder

Not so long ago, social anxiety in children and teenagers was considered just a minor problem that they would outgrow in time. We now know differently. Starting in the 1980s, researchers such as Dr. Liebowitz, this book's coauthor, began putting social anxiety disorder on the scientific map.

Before that, scientists had described related personality traits such as shyness and introversion, as well as mental disorders that involved being overanxious in general. However, it wasn't until 1980 that the standard diagnostic manual used by mental health professionals, called the *Diagnostic and Statistical Manual of Mental Disorders,* added a category called social phobia. Today the terms *social phobia* and *social anxiety disorder* are often used interchangeably.

For the most part, the idea of social anxiety disorder has gained rapid acceptance among professionals and the public alike. It's still challenged in some circles, though. Critics charge that the disorder is easily overdiagnosed, with medication prescribed for people who are really just shy or slightly anxious. Such abuses are a potential problem with any disease that becomes the focus of intense media attention and drug company advertising, the way social anxiety has in recent years. Yet most experts agree that social anxiety disorder is a very real condition that can cause very real suffering. Fortunately, when the disorder is carefully diagnosed and appropriately treated, the improvement is usually very real as well.

request for a date to the prom. Although the high school years are often described as carefree, they are not carefree for everyone. They certainly weren't for me.

If I had wholeheartedly believed then that my perceptions of social situations were skewed, that I wasn't the only one who felt this way, and that there were people who take this condition seriously, even appreciate the courage it requires to seek support, my teenage years might have turned out differently. Thanks to my journey, I was finally able to shed a new, healthier light on some of the misconceptions, embarrassment, and shame that unnecessarily weighed on my shoulders for years. At 27 years old, I finally turned the pages on that chapter of my life once and for all.

Chapter Two

Moving From Dis-ease to Disease

I recall walking through the automatic doors at the supermarket as a little girl, feeling a compelling urge to touch the
floor before my mother picked me up and propped me in the
seat of the shopping cart. I needed a plan, and the one I finally
hit upon was fixing my sandal while casually allowing my fingers
to brush the floor.

I don't remember feeling anxious back then. To the contrary,
I thought I was magic. By the time I was four years old, I was
controlling the world by touching supermarket floors, devel-
oping intricate lucky and unlucky
number systems, repeating memo-
rized lists of items without errors,
and not touching certain objects
while tapping others a specific number of times. I instinctively
kept these rituals secret. If I ever told a soul about them, I
might not be able to trust my powers again.

Never were my rituals more important than when riding in
a car. At a young age, I developed my own personal rules of the
road:

*I instinctively kept
these rituals secret.*

1. Be seated with the seat belt fastened before the driver sits.
2. Never touch the radio.
3. Never read.
4. Keep feet off the floor and wait for x number of cars to pass.
5. If a truck interrupts #4, start over.
6. Never allow certain songs to pop into your head.
7. Never let an arm touch the door.
8. Keep doors locked at all times.
9. It's okay to sing to oneself, but stop singing at the good parts.
10. Never sleep.

Yet even my best efforts failed to ward off the stress I felt as a helpless passenger. My father's recollection of a family vacation when I was nine years old typifies my reaction to riding in a car:

> She was crouched behind the front seat, head down, sitting on the floor, when I realized that her reactions to traffic were a little different than most. We were traveling through very rural New Brunswick when she asked me to slow down. Nine-year-olds don't usually ask their dads to slow down. As a sometimes not very sensitive guy, I finally realized that what her mom had been telling me was true. Emily's reactions weren't always typical. Most kids don't even notice traffic. Emily was terrified.
>
> —Dad

With habits such as these, you might think I would have been prone to obsessive-compulsive disorder (OCD), a mental disorder characterized by recurrent, uncontrollable obsessions or compulsions. Technically speaking, an obsession is an anxiety-provoking thought or mental image that intrudes into a person's mind again and again, no matter how hard he or she tries to shut it out. A compulsion is an act that the person feels driven to perform in response to the obsession. Often, these compulsive acts take the form of rigid rules and eccentric rituals that don't serve any rational purpose, but that nevertheless begin to take over the person's life.

Like social anxiety, OCD is considered an anxiety disorder, because it's rooted in excessive, long-lasting fear and worry. And on the surface, OCD certainly seemed to be the direction in which I was headed. In fact, before the age of ten, I wasn't socially anxious at all. I loved school. I loved people. I shared ideas, plans, jokes, and stories with my teachers. I went to birthday parties, joined Daisy Girl Scouts, and volunteered for everything that might earn me a gold star for my forehead. I was one of the most popular girls, if not the most popular girl, in my class.

Then a strange thing happened on the way to puberty. Suddenly, my anxiety was more about one particular thing: the threat of being scrutinized and criticized by other people. By fourth grade, social anxiety was already starting to take hold of my life.

One Person in Every 15

It's estimated that social anxiety disorder affects nearly 7% of U.S. adults. For many, as for me, the first signs appear in late childhood or early adolescence. At times, the intense anxiety starts suddenly after an embarrassing incident. Often, though, it takes root more gradually and insidiously.

Social anxiety disorder seems to be about equally common in women and men. However, females may be more likely than males to have certain types of social fears. For example, some studies suggest that more girls than boys may experience test anxiety or feel afraid of embarrassing themselves, turning red, having a panic attack, or being judged by others as "stupid," "weak," or "crazy." Yet the bottom line is that social anxiety disorder can strike anyone of either sex.

Genetics may play a role. In adults, some studies have found that those who have a close relative with social anxiety disorder are more likely than other adults to have the disorder themselves. In children and adolescents, studies of twins also have suggested that a tendency toward social anxiety may be inherited. But a tendency is all it is. This predisposition may lie dormant until it's awakened by

...the actual development of social anxiety seems to depend on the interplay between a person's genes and his or her environment.

stressful life experiences. So the actual development of social anxiety seems to depend on the interplay between a person's genes and his or her environment.

One way that genetics may influence social anxiety is through inherited temperament—genetically based personality traits that first show up early in life and tend to stay relatively stable for a long time. Some children just seem to be shyer and more timid than others from day one. As babies, they may cry frequently, and as toddlers, they may seem shy and fearful. Once they're school age, they may be noticeably slower than their classmates to warm up to new people and situations. The term *behavioral inhibition* refers to this pattern of timid, fearful behavior.

As you might expect, behaviorally inhibited children are more likely than average to grow up into socially anxious teenagers. But it's far from a sure thing. Many children who are shy by nature still get along well at home and school and never develop the kind of intense anxiety that interferes with their life. And some children are like me—they start out confident and outgoing, yet still develop crippling social anxiety by their teens. Clearly, temperament isn't all that matters.

The Biology of My Psychology

On a physical level, social anxiety disorder is based in brain processes that have gone awry. You're well aware of all the external changes that have occurred in your body since puberty. What you may not realize is that your brain has been changing just as dramatically. Among other things, these changes affect brain circuits involved in recognizing and expressing fear, anxiety, and other emotions. All this rewiring inside the brain could expose vulnerabilities that previously lay hidden, which is one reason why social anxiety might suddenly emerge in adolescence.

Scientists are still trying to pinpoint the exact brain circuits responsible for social anxiety. However, one part of the brain that seems to be crucial is the amygdala. This small structure plays a big role in emotional memory, especially where fear is concerned. In brain imaging studies, adults with social anxiety disorder had greater activity in the amygdala than nonanxious adults when shown pictures of faces or asked to speak in front of an audience. They also had an unusual pattern of activity in other parts of the brain that make up a system for evaluating social cues and deciding whether a threat is present. Researchers believe these areas of the brain may be overactive in people with social anxiety disorder. As a result, the brain sends out a "threat!" alarm even in harmless social situations.

Within the brain, messages are relayed from nerve cell to nerve cell by chemical messengers known as neurotransmitters. Without the right balance of neurotransmitters, activity inside the brain is skewed in unhealthy directions. These neurotransmitters are thought to play a role in anxiety disorders:

- Gamma-amino-butyric acid (GABA) inhibits the activity of nerve cells and seems to help quell anxiety.
- Serotonin helps regulate mood, sleep, appetite, and sexual drive. Low levels of serotonin have been linked to both anxiety and depression.
- Dopamine enables movement and also influences motivation and the perception of reality. Some research suggests a link between low dopamine and social anxiety disorder.

How Nurture Influences Nature

Genes and biology may plant the seeds of anxiety, but life experiences are what make it grow. Some social fears are learned by imitating others. If your parents act shy, withdrawn, or fearful in social situations, you may learn to act that way, too. Parents also may promote anxiety by being overly critical, at one extreme, or overly protective, at the other. In my case, Mom was quick to sense a medical emergency lurking behind every scrape, bump, bruise, or rash. But the way you were raised is just one of many factors that may contribute to social anxiety.

Genes and biology may plant the seeds of anxiety, but life experiences are what make it grow.

Life stress is another. When someone is subjected to cruel teasing, bullying, rejection, or ridicule and then goes on to develop social anxiety, the connection seems clear. But other types of stress—for example, physical or sexual abuse, failing a grade, dropping out of school, getting into trouble with the law, moving frequently, running away from home, or having parents who are separated or divorced—also may trigger social anxiety disorder in vulnerable teens. The more such factors you have in your life, the greater your risk seems to be.

Self-Fulfilling Prophesies

You're shaping your environment at the same time as it's shaping you. If you're socially anxious, you probably tend to distance yourself from others. While you may be doing this because you feel self-conscious and afraid of making a bad impression, to other people, your behavior may just seem arrogant and aloof. As a result, they may indeed end up rejecting or making fun of you, which just confirms your worst fears and increases your anxiety. It's a vicious cycle that I came to know all too well. But treatment helped me break free, and it can do the same for you.

Explanations don't always come easily, however. Looking back into my own past, I see vague clues rather than obvious reasons.

Growing Up in the "Perfect" Family

I was 26 years old and sitting across from my therapist when she asked whether my parents had a happy marriage. My first thought was, *of course*. My parents had been married 38 years, never separated, never even seriously considered the possibility of a divorce. They met and married in their mid-twenties, immediately began a family, and took on traditional roles that suited them to a tee.

In many ways, my childhood was ideal. Mom baked molasses cookies. Dad played *Daddy's Little Girl* and *Ten Good Years* on the piano. My three older sisters and I would stand beside him, singing the "womp, womp, womp" parts. My parents would read the travel section of *The New York Times* to one another and make up dream vacations. The whole family would go apple picking and dig potatoes in the garden together.

Ideal? It was unreal.

Like all parents, mine argued—sometimes loudly. Every so often, one would get angry enough to drive off for a few hours, but by dinnertime my mom, dad, sisters, and I would all be seated around the table, eating lasagna and making no mention of the incident. As the years passed, though, life around our house slowly changed. My grandmother came to live with us for a while, my oldest sisters went away to college, and the tension and distance in my parents' relationship seemed to grow. Distractions, such as family rides in the country and lunches out, were less frequent, and vacations together began to feel more like work than pleasure.

As a fourth grader, I could not fathom considering my life anything but the best. Half of the children of my generation were products of separated parents or broken homes. I could boast that my parents had been together 20-odd years. They were uncommonly traditional. Dad was the breadwinner and head of the household. Mom was the homemaker who took pride in her huge Italian meals. My three sisters were well-adjusted, popular, bright, and never in an inch of trouble. Weren't we perfect?

It took me 26 years to admit that we, like all families, were not.

First Cracks in the Façade

"I love you with all my chickens." I repeated this to my mother while she rolled out biscuits, when she drove to the grocery store, even as she brushed her teeth in the evenings. For some reason, it struck me as the ultimate endearment. And "loving with chickens" seemed like an apt way to describe our close relationship. Mom and I were certainly both chickens when it came to riding in cars, talking to strangers, and walking into brightly lit buildings.

While Mom and I would trade lighthearted endearments, Dad showed how he felt with deeds rather than words. He offered rides to the mall and fried up greasy stacks of his famous "cowboy sandwiches" when my mother was under the weather. He maintained the cars and the yard, tilled the garden, and kept out of his daughters' scuffles over who had borrowed whose lip gloss and wouldn't give it back. Outside the house, Dad was outgoing and struck others as perpetually happy—but then, we were all different on the outside than we were at home.

In our family, emotions were not shared, but interpreted. My mother exaggerated hers, my father hid his behind actions, and I claimed to be feeling whatever I thought would go over well. As the household grew more tense over time, the pattern was magnified, and we were all reduced to reading each other's signals and trying to interpret what someone *really* meant by what was said or done.

Meanwhile, fourth grade brought a new set of challenges. I was separated from my closest friends, who had been assigned the other classroom. It was difficult spending every class and every recess apart from my usual circle of girlfriends. At the same time, my ten-year-old classmates were changing. They were talking about pop stars, wearing brand-name sneakers, and trying out for soccer and softball teams. For the first time in my life, being different wasn't an asset.

For the first time in my life, being different wasn't an asset.

I wanted the more grown-up clothes, stylish haircuts, and mature lunch boxes that my friends had, but I kept silent. I didn't want to lose favor with the adults. I believed grown-ups liked me because I was a brainy, glasses-wearing, cute, round kid. I played the part of a child who parroted political arguments and denied inclinations to watch popular TV shows in favor of the evening news. I struggled through violin lessons in spite of not liking the instrument. Shaping myself into the person I believed other people wanted me to be had worked well in the past. It had made me a stand-out student. Now the friends who had fostered their own interests were blossoming into individuals, and I, still looking for outside approval, felt left behind.

Fourth Grade—How Mortifying!

In a matter of months, I became extremely sensitive to the impression I was making on others. I recall agonizing over a fourth-grade reflexive pronoun lesson in which I said "theirselves" instead of "themselves." I thought I was right. I'd always said "theirselves," and up until that moment, I'd always been good enough in language to know the answers offhand without having to study. When I realized that I had, in fact, made an error, a terrible, burning red shame came over me.

Then there was the incident of the "novel note." I had begun writing a novel in third grade—the story of a 10-year-old orphan forced to live with her wealthy and distant wheelchair-bound grandmother. It was sure to be published and make me famous. How could such a clever and original story not be adored by millions?

The novel grew and grew. I didn't show it to my family, fearing overblown praise or suggested changes. Instead, I proudly brought it to my teacher, Mrs. M. In my melodramatic fourth-grade fashion, I composed a note on the novel's first page explaining why Mrs. M. was the only one to whom I could show the book, because she was the sole person who understood me. Mrs. M. replied. She wrote that she was flattered, but urged me to give my parents a chance.

Immediately, I was mortified that I had written such a silly, exaggerated note. I ripped out the page and tossed it into the trash. After that, every time I opened the notebook and saw the first page missing, I was reminded of my humiliation, and I soon abandoned the novel. Even in high school, I still lacked the nerve to take peek inside the notebook that had once meant so much to me.

I will always remember fourth grade as the Year of the Novel Note. Yet this incident, which looms so large in my memory, was a complete nonevent in the lives of those around me. While I was fixated on my presumed humiliation, they were seeing me in a more realistic—and ironically, much less judgmental— light. Years later, when I asked my former music teacher what she remembered about me at that age, this is what she recalled:

> My earliest classroom memories are of you as a very creative fourth grader. One of my assignments was to have small groups write a short play, which was to be accompanied by music. I still remember how impressed I was with your imaginative writing!
>
> —Mrs. R.

My Fall From Social Grace

As a fifth-grader—no longer the most popular, sought-after girl—I began to doubt nearly everything I did. I fretted over my still-childish dress and flyaway hair. I was mortified if I made errors in class. Reading aloud became a nightmare, and I was consumed with dread for hours before each reading group.

Though I desperately wanted to be on top of everything, perfection proved impossible. I simply couldn't be the top student academically, athletically, musically, aesthetically, and socially. I was crushed to realize that many of my girlfriends were more fashionable, more athletic, better artists, better spellers, faster in math, and preferred by the boys in our class. I couldn't accept such changes as natural. It seemed as though

I must have done something very wrong. I felt as if I were being punished for taking pleasure in being a standout, acting bossy, and seeming conceited.

Instead of dusting myself off and gracefully accepting second, third, or eighth place, I dropped out of many activities. Unless I knew I was going to be very good at something, I didn't do it at all. Now I followed friends instead of taking the lead from time to time. By sixth grade, I'd lost rank in my clique altogether.

> Unless I knew I was going to be very good at something, I didn't do it at all.

Things only got worse in junior high. No longer was I invited to every slumber party or trip to the mall. *Who needs them anyway?* I asked myself. Those girls were weak, dependent, and

The Incredible Shrinking Worldview

Viewing the world through social anxiety is like looking through a telescope: your vision narrows, until all you can see is the perceived threat of embarrassment or humiliation. Over time, your constant dread of social situations can lead to considerable worry and distress. Some worry is a good thing, keeping you out of dangerous or inappropriate situations. But intense, uncontrollable worry only makes you miserable and holds you back from living life to its fullest.

Before long, you're likely to begin avoiding the situations that make you so uncomfortable. You may start giving up activities, turning down invitations to parties, or making excuses not to go to school, even though you're quite willing to do your schoolwork at home. Calling a classmate or striking up a conversation with a stranger may seem next to impossible. Eventually, you may find that you're spending more and more time by yourself and missing out on much of the fun that other people your age are having. Of course, everyone feels a little nervous and self-conscious now and then. But by the time you've reached this point, you may have crossed the line from ordinary anxiety to anxiety disorder.

needy. I, on the other hand, was strong, independent, and able to entertain myself. I desperately wanted to believe this version of reality. Needing friends to giggle with on the phone or pass notes to in science class was a sign of immaturity—wasn't it?

The truth was that I wanted to be included more than anything. In and out of school, I was forever thinking about connecting with the old clique. I dreamed of the day when the tables would turn back around in my favor.

It wasn't only the retreat from friends that was getting me down. I doubted my competency to do anything to the point of being unable to talk in complete sentences. I was forever backtracking, worrying that what I said five words earlier might have been interpreted in a way I didn't intend. I no longer knew how high to raise my hand in class, and asking to excuse myself to use the bathroom seemed like the most embarrassing task in the world. Every movement, from how I sat in a chair to how I brushed the hair out of my eyes, was painstakingly analyzed and planned.

This was more than teen angst. It was the start of social anxiety disorder.

Chapter Three

Not Just Another Shy Teenager

I am going to be so cool . . . I won't know what struck me. I am going to be talkative and energetic. I think I can do it if I try really, really hard. I want to try out the new me, the new talkative and energetic person I am going to be. I can do it if I try. I'll leave my fears behind and be popular. I'll have to call people. I can do that. I hope.

—Diary entry, September 7, 1992, the last day of summer vacation before eighth grade

I get so frustrated when S. treats me so badly! . . . I'm so upset, but why should I care? I'm not close with her. AND I DON'T WANT TO BE EITHER! She was acting oh so discrete when she asked C. to her house to spend the night. S. pulls her aside and starts talking in a low whisper in front of me. I knew what she was saying. I wouldn't want to go to her house anyway! I'm NOT jealous. I was angry because she was acting as though C. was one of the privileged few. "S., I know what you're saying," I tell her. "Can't you say it out loud? It only makes me feel weird when you whisper." She retaliated with a "well, geez Emily. I didn't want

to...” What? Hurt my feelings? I never go to her house, why
would I be invited this time?

—Diary entry, April 23, 1993,
near the end of eighth grade

By eighth grade, social anxiety was pushing me farther and
farther into the background at school. Over the next few years,
I gradually disappeared altogether.

A Day in the Life of Nobody

Fast-forward to a winter morning three years later. I awoke to
the rumble of snowplows in the distance. Rolling toward the
window, I cupped my hand over the glass, hoping there had
been a huge snowfall overnight, but there was nothing but a
thin white film on the road and the sad acceptance that school
would carry on as usual.

I fell back onto my pillow, feeling the familiar pangs of
dread crawl through my stomach. In a few minutes, my mother
would come knocking on my bedroom door and tell me it was
time to get ready for another day of eleventh grade. It was the
same routine as yesterday, the day
before yesterday, and the day before that.

*...please don't let this
be the day when everyone
finds out I'm crazy.*

"Please, God, please let this be
the day I'm different," I groaned.
Maybe that was asking too much.
"At least, please don't let this be the day when everyone finds
out I'm crazy."

Everything about school tied my stomach into knots. The
air smelled like a mix of floor wax and hot lunch. The over-
head lights and vending machines hummed incessantly. Every

fixture from the trophy cases to the plastic desks seemed cold and uninviting. The cheerleaders had taped huge red-and-white posters to the walls promoting school spirit. How anyone could feel a cheery connection to such a dreary building was completely beyond me.

I was always one of the first students to arrive, never daring to risk being a few minutes late. I stood at my lonely post in the school lobby, feeling conspicuous and wishing there was a crowd into which I could fade. The teachers trickled in next. I escaped their glances by digging around in my purse. Nothing could have been a worse start to the day than a teacher's well-intentioned "good morning." I assumed the friendly greeting was really condescending pity for the girl who showed up at school ten minutes before everyone else.

The other students arrived in groups of three or four, talking about last night's basketball game or comparing answers to trigonometry problems. I was in awe of the ease with which they moved. They knew how to do what I did not—how to wear the perfect outfit, how to nonchalantly drop their book bags at their feet, and how to casually move florescent gum from one cheek to the other. They knew everything. They knew how to be normal.

I wandered up to my old clique, saying just enough to earn the right to stand among them. I asked a question about the science assignment. I complimented someone's shoes. I squeezed myself into a space in the circle, but I had long ago ceased to be part of the group. The girls who used to be my best friends were now only acquaintances. They didn't exactly ignore me. But they didn't acknowledge me, either.

I attempted to speak, but the words caught in my throat. I was sure my voice sounded childish, and I foresaw rolled eyes and bored reactions to what I wanted to say. By the time I had finally settled upon the words I wanted to speak and the voice I intended to use, the moment had long since passed, and everyone had moved on to a new subject. I swallowed the unused words and blinked back tears.

Another morning's high hopes for being a brand-new person had once again fallen flat by 8:30 A.M.

Up to My Ears in Dread

Finally, the bell rang. Boys zoomed behind pretty girls, stopped short, said something funny, then ran. Girls talked, bumped shoulders, and whispered secrets to one another. Alone in the crowd, I raised my head and gripped my bag determinedly. I'd prove that I wasn't an outcast. I pretended as though something ten feet ahead had caught my eye. Then I smiled and hurried to catch up with an imaginary friend lost somewhere in the crush of students.

In first-period chemistry, I was up to my ears in dread—dread of having to say "here" when my name was called, of getting back yesterday's assignment, of looking as if I didn't fit in. I glanced around the room to compare my notebook, pencils, clothes, jewelry, hairstyle, backpack, and pile of textbooks with everyone else's. The corners of my notebook lacked the lazy scribbles from a friend. My clothes were my sister's hand-me-downs. And there were definitely too many books stacked in front of me.

The imagined thoughts of my classmates bombarded me from all sides: "Her hair is so ugly." "Yeah, but did you see those yellow teeth?" "Look at what she's wearing." "She's covered in cat hair." "She's covered in her own hair. Did you see her arms?" "She better not be my lab partner."

Meanwhile, Mrs. H. set a pile of graded papers on the edge of her desk, ready to return them to the class. *What did she think of my answers?* I wondered. *Were they silly, messy, too long, too short, too precise, or just plain wrong? Did my work look like I was trying too hard or not hard enough?*

I tried to read Mrs. H.'s face quickly, without making eye contact. I was sure every suggestion she made to the class was aimed squarely at me: "You must be neater. You must check your answers. You must take more time with your homework. You must always use blue or black ink." Me, me, me, me. "You must ask questions if you don't understand an assignment." Definitely me.

My day only got worse in math class. Mr. C. held us past the bell to drill for a quiz. I tried to concentrate, but all I could think about was getting to the cafeteria. I *had* to grab a seat at my regular table before it filled up and left me odd man out.

As soon as we were dismissed, I hurried to the cafeteria. But to my horror, someone had slung a jacket over the back of my usual chair. No one cared that there was no room for me. I briefly considered asking if I could squeeze in, but just as quickly ruled that out. Every cough, sideways glance, or raised eyebrow would be a message that I was uninvited. Miserable and humiliated, I pulled up a chair to the end of a nearby table.

The embarrassment stayed with me throughout the afternoon. When it was time to talk in French class about how I had spent the previous evening, I responded, "J'ai fais mes devoirs"—"I did my homework." Others in the class had "regardé la télévision" with friends, "ont mangé à McDonald's" or "sont allées au cinéma" with their dates. I had nervo uttered something about homework in the most inelegant French ever spoken. Under my sleeve, I dug my nails into the skin of my wrist—hard. The more it hurt, the more relief I felt as I tried to shut out my emotional pain with the physical variety.

Criteria for Social Anxiety Disorder

I didn't know it then, but I was well on my way to becoming the poster girl for social anxiety disorder. When professionals diagnose this disorder, they look for an extreme, persistent fear of one or more social situations. To qualify as social anxiety, these situations must involve either being around unfamiliar people or being exposed to possible scrutiny by others.

> When professionals diagnose this disorder, they look for an extreme, persistent fear of one or more social situations.

Everyone feels a little shy or self-conscious now and then. But people with social anxiety disorder are afraid that they'll act in a way that leads to embarrassment or humiliation, and they take

Pushing the Panic Button

...acks that are triggered by specific events such as public ...n be part of social anxiety disorder. However, panic at- ...me on unexpectedly may be caused by a different ... as panic disorder. People with panic disorder fear ...k without warning, so they worry about getting ...ere they can't easily get away, such as riding ... social anxiety disorder was my primary ...vhen my behavior had some features of

that fear to an irrational, dysfunctional level. As a result, they become very anxious in the social situations they fear.

In some cases, the anxiety gets so bad that it leads to a full-blown panic attack—a sudden, unexpected wave of intense fear and apprehension that's accompanied by physical symptoms, such as a racing or pounding heart, shortness of breath, sweating, trembling, chest pain, nausea, or choking sensations. In other cases, the symptoms may be milder but longer lasting. For example, a teenager might worry about attending an upcoming dance for days or weeks beforehand. Afterward, that same teen might spend days agonizing over every little thing he did (or failed to do) at the dance.

The Culture Paradox

Nature and nurture both play a role in social anxiety disorder. This disorder is found in all types of cultures—strong evidence for its genetic and biological roots. But the particular way in which social anxiety is experienced also is partly shaped by the culture in which a person lives.

Researchers talk about the difference between group-focused and individually focused countries. In group-focused countries such as Japan and South Korea, social harmony is the top priority and social rules tend to be well defined and rigidly enforced. On the other hand, in individually focused countries such as the United States, Australia, and the Netherlands, individual achievement is the top priority and social rules are generally a bit looser.

Group-focused societies tend to be *less* tolerant of behavior that makes other people uncomfortable. In such cultures, people with social anxiety disorder often have unrealistic fears about such things as having a gaze that others will find too penetrating or a body odor that others will find offensive. In contrast, group-focused societies may be *more* tolerant of shy or withdrawn behavior, because they aren't so focused on individual ambition and success.

Any way you slice it, social anxiety isn't much fun. To escape the misery, people may start avoiding the feared social situations, or they may endure these situations only with great dread or distress. The avoidance, dread, or distress, in turn, begins interfering seriously with their lives. They may have trouble keeping up with their daily routine or maintaining social relationships. Or they may have problems getting along at school or work. People with social anxiety disorder are well aware that their fear is excessive or unreasonable, but they feel powerless to rein it in. By this point, the fear is controlling them, not the other way around.

Red Flags to Watch For

Are you starting to wonder whether you might have social anxiety disorder? Below are some warning signs to watch for. Taken alone, some of these signs may indicate nothing more than ordinary shyness or self-consciousness, especially if they're not causing you much trouble or distress. But the more signs you have, and the more disruptive or upsetting they are, the more likely it is that you might need help:

In general

- Excessive concern about being judged by others or embarrassing yourself
- Worrying for days before an upcoming social event
- Fretting about your social missteps for days afterward
- Confusion or freezing in social situations
- Frequent nervous blushing, trembling, or sweating
- Difficulty with public speaking
- Distress over being the center of attention

- Unwillingness to invite friends to get together
- Reluctance to start conversations or make phone calls
- Avoiding eye contact with other people
- Staying home from social events
- Feeling like an outsider in group situations

At school

- Avoiding speaking in class or making presentations
- Not speaking up or taking part in group activities
- Sitting alone regularly in the cafeteria or library
- Reluctance to write on the board or read aloud
- Hesitance to play sports in front of other people
- Fear of performing in a play or concert before an audience
- Excessive anxiety over taking tests in class
- Constant worry about being judged by the teacher

Social anxiety disorder isn't something that comes and goes overnight. In fact, in young people under age 18, having symptoms for at least six months is one of the diagnostic signs that professionals look for. Without treatment, the disorder occasionally becomes less troublesome or goes away on its own in adulthood. Often, though, it lasts a lifetime, rising and falling with changing life demands. For example, a teenager who's terrified of talking in front of the class at school might no longer be bothered by that fear after graduation, but her fear might later resurface with a vengeance if she gets a job that requires public speaking.

Yet people with social anxiety disorder don't have to just suffer in silence. Treatment can help them overcome their fears and get on with enjoying life. And if new problems crop up

Shyness or Something More?

There's nothing unusual about feeling a little embarrassed when you don't know the answer in class or having your palms get clammy the first time you speak to a cute classmate. But if you're still fretting over the incident days later, and if you're so worried about it happening again that you start dreading class and avoiding your classmates, you might be on the road to social anxiety. Here are some other examples to help you tell the difference between ordinary shyness or self-consciousness, on one hand, and social anxiety disorder, on the other.

Shyness or Self-Consciousness	Social Anxiety Disorder
You spend hours working up the nerve to ask a classmate to prom.	You spend days trying to work up the nerve to ask a classmate to prom. Finally, you give up and decide that you didn't really want to go anyway.
You spend an hour choosing what to wear on the first day of school.	You spend an hour choosing what to wear on the first day of school. Then you spend the whole day second-guessing your choice and worrying about what other people think of your appearance.
You blush when called upon unexpectedly in class.	You blush when called upon unexpectedly in class. Over the next several weeks, you start making excuses to miss that class as often as possible. When you do show up, you keep your head down, hoping the teacher won't notice you.
You love to play basketball, so you try out for the team, even though you're nervous about how you'll do.	You love to play basketball, but you don't try out for the team, because you can't face the possibly of not making the cut.

later, they'll be prepared. They'll know what to do and where to turn for help when they need it.

Unfortunately, no one told me then what I'm telling you now. I had to learn all my lessons the painful way.

And It Just Keeps Getting Worse

By eleventh grade, I had stopped receiving invitations. It hurt to look on as the other girls made "call me" gestures to one another when leaving the school building. It was the ache that ended every school day.

At home on the weekend, I daydreamed about returning to school on Monday morning with a new-and-improved, outgoing personality. Everyone would love me, and I'd have boyfriends like you wouldn't believe. But Monday inevitably came, and all hope faded as I stood alone again in the lobby. Teachers arrived, and I despaired. Students followed, and my heart sank further as I listened to them casually talk on about their fabulous weekends.

It didn't matter that I was class secretary and president of the French club. I assumed that I had landed those offices by default. When a local TV station highlighted me as student of the week, it only broadcast to the tri-county area that Emily was now a regionally recognized nerd.

By senior year, I had given up completely on clubs and Friday night dances. Despite dreams of a career in theater, I quit band and chorus, too. And I was the only one in my class not to fly to Disney World for the senior class trip. I assumed my fear of planes would seem like a pathetic ploy for attention, and I dreaded having to team up with roommates who would undoubtedly cringe at the thought of rooming with me. The trip would be a 96-hour ordeal, from amusement park rides to bathroom stops to getting a seat on the bus. It seemed simpler to stay home.

The more I avoided, the worse my social anxiety became. Skipping one dance made it easier to skip the next, and each time only strengthened my assumption that I'd make a fool of myself if I ever went to a dance again. By opting out, I never

Allowed to grow freely, untested by real-world experiences, my fears quickly mushroomed out of control.

challenged the belief that everyone thought I was unappealing, awkward, and inept. Rather than risk blatant rejection, it seemed easier to believe that I was unable to be liked and incapable of fitting in. Allowed to grow freely, untested by real-world experiences, my fears quickly mushroomed out of control.

Chapter Four

First Steps Toward Recovery

F or years, I was caught in a web of what-ifs: What if people think I'm exaggerating? What if it seems that I'm only after attention? What if my anxiety is something that will go away on its own? What if it's not and I'm sent to a mental hospital? What if all my anxiety is actually due to a personality flaw—something I could fix if I were stronger, braver, kinder, and altogether a better person?

Name any television series that had a therapist as a character and was on the air or in reruns when I was a teenager, and I've probably seen it—*The Bob Newhart Show*, *M*A*S*H*, even the animated *Dr. Katz, Professional Therapist*. Any series that depicted psychological problems fascinated me, and I jealously watched as the Hollywood therapists treated patients with kindness and compassion. I tried to hide my keen interest in these scenes from others, ashamed of what it seemed to reveal about my own emotional state. I kept a tight grip on the remote, and if anyone walked into the room—*click!* I'd switch to the home-shopping channel.

Today I realize that my fascination was nothing more than a sign that I wanted help. I desperately longed for someone to listen to me and take me seriously. Behind closed doors, I fantasized about conversations with the dedicated therapists from these TV shows. In my imagined sessions, the therapists always were concerned, took me seriously, and never insinuated that I might be exaggerating.

In my heart, I knew that my anxiety warranted a visit to a real-life mental health professional, but I never let on to others how badly I was hurting. Anxiety and depression seemed too shameful to mention to my parents, who politely ignored my moodiness as if it didn't exist. The fear of having my problems belittled or hearing someone tell me that I was "just shy" kept me locked in needless silence for years.

I believed that I wore my emotions on my sleeve for the whole world to see. So why didn't anyone notice? Didn't anyone care? It seemed impossible for people *not* to notice my torment, when everything from walking across a room to getting a drink of water was so excruciating for me.

It seemed impossible for people not to notice my torment...

There were times when I was glad to be shaking, red, or teary-eyed, because I hoped someone would reach out and offer to help. When they didn't, I concluded that no one wanted to help me because I must be exaggerating my emotions for attention.

It wasn't until I became a teacher myself that I realized how difficult it is to see into students' minds. My former teacher Mrs. W. confirmed this impression when I went to see her on the return trip to my old school:

I regarded Emily as a seasoned traveler as she had spent part of the summer in France the year before. As a result, I assumed the overnight flight was uneventful as most of the students slept or talked anxiously about the upcoming week. During lunch about the third day, my husband and I sat with Emily and noticed that the back of her hands had started to scab over; it looked like she had fallen. When we asked her what she had done, she quickly put her hands under the table in her lap and said it happened on the flight over. She was so nervous that she dug her nails into the back of her hands to get through the night. I felt terrible that I had not checked on her, but again assumed all was well because she never complained and none of the other students sitting next to her said anything . . . Teenage anxiety is a tough part of teaching. One doesn't want to get too personal or make students feel uncomfortable by commenting on or asking about their uneasiness. In school we have counselors, but we have no class in how to survive teenage angst.

—Mrs. W.

The One With More Breakage

At my high school, there was a team-building club, and I joined in hopes of showing people a bolder, better side of me. I was tired of being seen as the one who "had more breakage" (my chemistry teacher's term), or the one who never drove over 40 miles per hour in driver's education. Maybe I could break out of being "the only introvert in the class" and "too antisocial" (more teacher terms) by signing up for this popular club.

Once a year, the team-building club would head out to the forest to climb trees, trek blindfolded through the woods, and swing down zip lines. Then at the end of the day, the group would get together to answer questions that were designed to help everyone get to know each other on a deeper level. Out loud, I claimed to think it was all too touchy-feely, but deep down, I relished the idea that I would be as vital to the group as anyone else, at least theoretically.

Late one evening, we were herded into cabins to answer personal questions read to us from index cards. We were left to ourselves, but I secretly wished a teacher had stayed in the room to hear my responses. Teachers, I thought, had the ability to read between the lines. If only a teacher could hear my honest answers, maybe he or she would notice that something was really wrong.

"What makes you cry?" I reclined on a bunk, waiting for my chance to answer, rehearsing the words I planned to say over and over in my head. Some people talked about deaths in the family. Others mentioned breakups. Then it was my turn.

"I cry when I'm embarrassed."

Someone snorted. A pause followed, and that was it. The question rolled to the next person. Another question was posed, but I opted to pass. I also passed the next time, then the next until the activity was over. The chance to let my classmates get to know the real me had passed.

Biting the Hand That Helps You

Perhaps the closest I came to finding an advocate in high school was Mrs. R., my after-school voice teacher. She took a genuine interest in me, and she told me repeatedly not to say "I'm sorry" so often. Of course, that only made me want to say "I'm sorry" more, hoping that we would have a conversation about it.

I remember one day when Mrs. R. stopped playing the piano and looked up at me curiously. "I think *you* think people expect things from you," she said. "*Do* you believe that?"

I choked back tears. Although I quickly shook my head no, I began to look forward to each and every voice lesson after that. I appreciated Mrs. R.'s concern, but around other people, I pretended not to like her—to hate her, in fact. During my junior year, I accused Mrs. R. of being too intrusive. After that, I didn't sign up for a fourth year of voice, and I abandoned all hope of getting help at school.

It takes a special teacher to invest personal interest in a student. Had I spoken up to Mrs. R. in seventh, ninth, or eleventh grade, I might have saved myself years of turmoil. Instead, I remained silent. It's a well-known rule in the student code: Those who turn to a teacher for help with personal problems are fair game for ridicule. I chose to suffer in silence rather than risk the shame.

Moving Beyond High School

High school graduation came and went with little fanfare. Though there were probably several nice sentiments written in my yearbook, the only two phrases I remembered were "you were a girl I never really talked to" and "we grew apart." One evening, I sat on my bedroom floor and tearfully tore the pages into tiny strips so thin that not one word remained legible.

Later that summer, the university I planned to attend sent notification that my single dorm room had been changed to a double. I immediately withdrew and enrolled at a local college where I could retain the privacy of my own bedroom. Yet despite this disappointment, I resolved to make a fresh start. Emily the College Freshman would be a brand-new person.

You can probably guess what happened next. Some new outfits and a change of scenery didn't magically transform me into the confident, outgoing person I wanted to be. When I wasn't in class, I hid in forgotten corners of the library. Day after day, I'd sit at my partitioned desk, eat a cello-wrapped brownie from the vending machine, and read the

Some new outfits and a change of scenery didn't magically transform me into the confident, outgoing person I wanted to be.

same book on anxiety over and over until I knew every word by heart. I would never check it out, however. I was sure the librarian would look first at the title, then at me, and laugh to herself about how much I needed it.

There was no doubt in my mind that I had an anxiety disorder, but I didn't believe that professional help was an option for me. The success stories in the book featured well-to-do people with the financial means to go to the best doctors. I told myself that no one in real life got that kind of treatment. Real people didn't have family and friends pressing them to see world-renowned therapists.

Then one afternoon, my psychology professor called me to his desk to ask if I was depressed. He reassured me that it wasn't obvious, but explained that he had experience identifying the signs and apparently I fit the bill. I desperately wanted to say "yes," but I couldn't squeeze the word from my throat, so instead I nervously shook my head "no." Those old what ifs resurfaced with a vengeance: What if I admitted to feeling depressed? Would it seem like a pathetic ploy for attention? Would I be told to seek professional help? What if I said "yes" but the professional said "no way"?

The professor then asked another question: "Are you shy?" I tentatively nodded "yes" to that one. He offered to lend me books on the subject from his office, but as much as I wanted to accept his offer, I never did. Rather than taking this active step, I chose the passive route. I strategically positioned myself in places where he might see me between classes, hoping that he'd approach me again, maybe insist that I walk with him to his office. But he never did.

The opportunity wasn't totally lost, though. Soon after, the professor began calling me to the front of the classroom to ask me off-the-wall questions, trying to ease my nervousness by forcing me to confront my fears. After the final exam, he thanked me for being a good sport, but it was I who should have thanked him. An honest-to-goodness psychologist thought I might be depressed. Maybe I would be taken seriously if I ever had the nerve to ask for help.

Two Disorders for the Price of One

My professor's instincts had been spot on. I *did* have depression along with my social anxiety. That might make me sound like the unluckiest girl in the world, but as it turns out, it's not that unusual to have two or more mental disorders at the same time. Following are brief descriptions of some common co-morbid conditions—in other words, disorders that frequently occur side-by-side with social anxiety disorder:

- *Depression* is a disorder that involves being in a low mood nearly all the time, or losing interest or enjoyment in almost everything. People with depression typically feel sad, empty, and hopeless, but teenagers sometimes feel irritable instead. These feelings last for at least two weeks, are associated with other mental and physical symptoms, and cause significant distress or problems in everyday life. As a group, young people with anxiety disorders are eight times more likely than those without the disorders to suffer from depression.
- *Substance abuse* is another common problem among young people with social anxiety disorder, who may try to find instant relief in alcohol or drugs. Unfortunately, this strategy doesn't work, and they just end up creating more problems for themselves. Substance abuse increases the risk of declining grades, car crashes and other accidents, unprotected sex, physical and

sexual assault, health problems, suicide, and death from overdose. It also can lead to legal problems associated with illicit drugs, underage drinking, or driving under the influence.

- *Eating disorders* may be associated with social anxiety disorder, too, although the exact nature of this link is still being investigated. One large study published in the *American Journal of Psychiatry* in 2004 found that about 20% of people with an eating disorder had also experienced social anxiety disorder at some point in their lives. This held true for both anorexia nervosa and bulimia nervosa (commonly known as anorexia and bulimia). People with anorexia have an intense fear of becoming fat, so they severely restrict what they eat, often to the point of near-starvation. People with bulimia binge on large quantities of food, then purge by forced vomiting, laxative or diuretic use, or excessive exercise. Some researchers have suggested that an extreme concern about being judged might set the stage for an unhealthy preoccupation with body weight.

People with social anxiety disorder sometimes have other anxiety disorders as well. For example, they might also have generalized anxiety disorder, which is characterized by constant worry over a number of different things. Or they might have a specific phobia, which is characterized by intense fear that is focused on a particular animal, object, or situation and that is out of proportion to

People with social anxiety disorder sometimes have other anxiety disorders as well.

any real threat. My fear of flying is an example of a specific phobia.

Having two or more disorders definitely doesn't mean you're a lost cause, but it does mean you have twice as much to gain by getting treatment as soon as possible. Yet despite all the signs pointing toward a need for help, I stalled a bit longer.

Inching Toward Professional Help

My sophomore year, I transferred to another college, determined to start over yet again with new clothes and a new attitude. The fervor didn't last. In a matter of weeks, I had stopped leaving my dorm room except when absolutely necessary. I did nothing but pour over schoolwork, sleep, and cry.

More and more, I thought about what my former psychology professor had said. Maybe there *were* resources available. I knew there was a counseling center at the school, but people didn't really go there, did they?

I began frequenting Internet chat rooms on depression, where I found other people with symptoms similar to mine. Although turning to the Internet was a way of keeping my distance, it opened my eyes to the throngs of ordinary people who were already getting treatment. Many had been prescribed medications, and others were receiving therapy. Some talked openly about subjects such as self-injury and thoughts of suicide—subjects that I had believed no one actually mentioned aloud.

The chat rooms showed me that I wasn't alone. If I were to tell someone how I was feeling, I might be taken at my word. Better yet, I might not be sent to a mental institution if I admitted that, in my more distressed moments, I'd scraped my legs with scissors and occasionally contemplated suicide.

If You Ever Feel Like Hurting Yourself

Suicide is the third leading cause of death among young people between the ages of 15 and 24. Some studies have found that young people with social anxiety disorder have an even higher-than-average risk of suicidal thoughts and behavior, while other studies have found no increase in risk. But it just makes sense that the stress of living in constant anxiety could tip the scales toward suicidal thoughts for some vulnerable individuals.

If you ever find yourself thinking about suicide or feeling the urge to hurt yourself, take action right away:

- *Tell someone you trust.* It's best to choose an older person—such as a parent, doctor, school counselor, school nurse, or religious advisor—who has more experience to draw upon when handling this type of situation.
- *Seek professional help.* Suicidal thoughts are an urgent symptom that needs immediate attention. If you're already in treatment, call your psychiatrist or therapist. If not, ask a trusted adult to help you find mental health care.
- *Call for help and hope.* Another source of immediate, 24-hour assistance is the National Suicide Prevention Lifeline (800-273-TALK).

As the weeks passed, my isolation, depression, and anxiety grew progressively worse. By the fall of my sophomore year, I had reached a breaking point. I felt utterly hopeless. Academics had long been the one thing that gave me a sense of purpose and self-esteem, but I was rapidly losing all interest in completing assignments. There was nothing left. I had no close friends, and I fought constantly with my parents.

One evening, I was going out to dinner when I felt a sudden rush of panic. To this day, I'm not sure exactly what happened. The panic could have been brought on by social anxiety, or it could have been a spontaneous attack like the ones that occur in panic disorder. At the time, I didn't stop to analyze it. I just

A Word About Cyber-Support

Internet chat rooms and online discussion boards may be less threatening than face-to-face conversations for many people with social anxiety disorder. As a result, these resources can be a good way to get the social support you crave, especially while you're still thinking about seeking help or are in the early stages of treatment. Just keep in mind that the same anonymity that's so appealing to you may also be attractive to unscrupulous types with more on their minds than chatting. These tips can help protect you online:

- Never give out personal information, such as your full name, home address, phone number, password, credit card number, or names of family members.
- Choose a chat room nickname that's different from your screen name or email address. That way, if you ever become uncomfortable with an online situation, you can exit the chat room and not worry that someone might track you down later.
- Don't believe everything you read. The people you meet online are like those in the offline world: Some are honest and credible, but others aren't. It can be harder to tell who's reliable and who isn't when you don't have face-to-face clues.
- Limit online friendships to cyberspace. Meeting offline is risky, because you never know for sure who is really typing out those chat room messages.

hurried back to my room, locked the door, slid to the ground, and stayed there. I wound up spending the whole evening crouched on the floor. I resolved to ask my parents about seeing a doctor. What did I have to lose? Even if they doubted me or blew off my request, I could feel no emptier or more alone than I already did.

Back home for Thanksgiving break not long afterward, I volleyed between being argumentative and feeling lethargic. Then out of the blue, I stopped my mother as we passed each other in the dining room. "Do you think maybe I could go get some medication for this?"—"this" being my ambiguous term for depression and anxiety.

"Of course," she replied.

And that was that. After some low-voiced conversations with my father, my mother made an appointment for me. Three weeks later, I was sitting in a psychiatrist's office. I was where I had dreamed of being for nearly a decade, and all it had taken to bring me to this moment was one passing comment in the dining room.

Three Barriers, and How to Overcome Them

Looking back, it's tempting to kick myself for not asking for help sooner. But reaching out wasn't easy. In general, getting mental health care as a young person requires three things: You need to believe that treatment is out there. You must be willing to accept treatment when it's offered. And you need to have adults on your side who believe that you could benefit from getting professional help. It took me a while to get all three of these ducks in a nice, neat row.

If you're having trouble believing in and accepting treatment, I hope this book—particularly the next two chapters—will change your mind. Remember that the sooner you take this step, the sooner you can start feeling better. It might help to have a family member or friend come along to the first appointment for moral support. Your support person will probably stay in the waiting room, but just knowing that he or she is out there can be a source of strength and reassurance.

It might help to have a family member or friend come along to the first appointment for moral support.

If you're looking for an adult to help you find care, a parent or guardian is usually your best bet. Not all parents are informed about or comfortable with mental illness, however. Other possible allies include another older relative or your family doctor, teacher, school counselor, or religious advisor. For information about the resources in your community, you can also contact your local mental health center or the local chapter of a national self-help organization. (A list of such organizations can be found in the Resources appendix at the end of this book.)

At Last, a Diagnosis

When I walked into the psychiatrist's office, I was a blank slate. Dr. A. didn't know me through my parents or my classmates. He didn't know where I had grown up, how well I did in school, or what kinds of incidents from my past had caused me deep embarrassment. He simply listened, and while I didn't speak with flowing ease, I had a feeling that my halting speech was fine with him.

I told Dr. A. that I thought I might be depressed, although I didn't explain why in detail or bring up the anxiety at all. He asked me a series of questions, and I recognized them as similar to those in the book on anxiety that I had read during my first year in college. "Emily," he said, "the score that indicates you might have social anxiety disorder is a 19. You scored a 47."

One might not think a high score on a test of mental disorders would be something to celebrate, but I couldn't have been happier. I wasn't making it up! I actually had an anxiety disorder as well as moderate depression. When Dr. A. asked if I had allergies to any medications, I felt further vindicated. I was going to be prescribed something. It was real. *It was real.*

I was fortunate. The first mental health professional I consulted picked up on my social anxiety disorder right away. As I've since come to realize, not everyone is so lucky, because social anxiety disorder isn't always easy to diagnose. It can't be detected with a blood test or seen on an X-ray. Instead, the professional must rely on asking you questions about your past history and current symptoms. At times, your parents might be asked to supply information as well.

To differentiate normal shyness and self-consciousness from an actual disorder, the professional will look for evidence that your symptoms are disrupting your daily life or causing serious distress. In addition, the professional will be alert for signs that you're having trouble bouncing back from ordinary stresses and strains. There's nothing unusual about blushing when you give a wrong answer in class. What *is* a concern is fretting about the incident for days or worrying so much about it happening again that you start making excuses to stay home from school.

Dr. A. was a psychiatrist, a medical doctor who specializes in the diagnosis and treatment of mental illnesses and emotional problems. However, social anxiety disorder also can be diagnosed and treated by other mental health professionals, including psychologists, clinical social workers, psychiatric nurses, and mental health counselors. Many people with social anxiety disorder wind up having two treatment providers: a psychiatrist or other doctor who prescribes and monitors medication, and another professional who provides psychotherapy.

The Social Anxiety Poster Child

By my third visit, Dr. A. had labeled me the "social anxiety poster child." Yet I was already feeling better. I was talking in class, asking for things in stores, and getting along better with my family. While I still had a long way to go, some of the drudgery of everyday tasks had been lifted from my shoulders, and I felt a surge of new energy. It made me wonder how severe my anxiety and depression must have been if a little pill could take away so much despair so quickly.

It wasn't a miraculous fix. One-on-one conversations and telephone calls were still torture, and I continued to prefer solitude over a trip to the local coffeehouse with other students from my floor. Over time, the novelty of answering questions in class began to wear off, too. I found myself once again focusing more on the charts in my textbooks and less on the professors' faces.

Maybe I expected too much, I thought. I considered going back to the psychiatrist and explaining that I was having trouble again, but I rejected that idea. Compared to what I had been through before, this discomfort was mild. It might seem that I was naively expecting miracles.

A year passed. The medicine had started to make me feel empty. I once enjoyed spurts of creativity and excitement, but the pills took that away. Now everything was so-so, bland, and blah. I recall thinking that I would prefer misery over feeling nothing at all. Rather than talking the problem over with Dr. A., though, I simply stopped taking the pills and ceased going to my monthly appointment. As a result, my life took a dramatic turn, this time for the decidedly worse.

Chapter Five

A Long Road Filled With Potholes

knew he was looking at me, but I wouldn't look up. Then I heard his voice: "What is it about yourself that you don't want anyone to know?"

I don't want people to find out that I'm crazy. The answer came to mind as soon as he asked the question, but I couldn't bring myself to say it out loud. Instead, I kept my eyes locked on the base of Dr. A.'s floor lamp and shrugged as if to say, "I don't know. You tell me. What don't I want anyone to know?"

A psychiatrist, not a psychic, Dr. A. suggested I go home and think about it.

Even if I had mustered the courage to utter the words aloud, I doubted Dr. A. or anyone else would have understood what I was feeling. I was convinced that I had lost my mind. Lately, I felt powerless to temper my moods, and my reactions sometimes seemed to veer out of control. One day, I was gung-ho about a new plan to travel the world. The next week, I wanted to spend huge sums of money on a brand-new wardrobe. A week after that, I was too depressed to care whether or not I had combed my hair in the last four days. I feared that I had the potential to do something self-destructive without realizing at the time how risky it was. But I was even more afraid of sharing this fear, so I remained a prisoner of my silence.

I feared that I had the potential to do something self-destructive without realizing at the time how risky it was.

Laid Low by Depression

When I was 15, I embarked on a pattern of looking for fresh starts in faraway places. I was convinced that spending the summer in France as an exchange student would be a golden opportunity to break out of my awkward stage. I was sure that I would return home six weeks later as a self-assured, worldly creature. Needless to say, I didn't.

Yet six years later, I was ready to try again, opting to spend a college semester studying in Paris. I boarded in an apartment overlooking the Champs Elysées, the city's famously romantic avenue lined with lovely gardens and rows of majestic trees. But despite the beauty of my surroundings, the discomfort of residing with a stranger consumed me. I passed my time studying on park benches in an effort to avoid sharing a living space. Three weeks into the trip, I decided to return to the United States. My plane landed at Newark less than 48 hours later.

Once home, I collapsed on the sofa and remained buried under a pile of blankets for over two weeks. In the past, depression had seemed to affect mainly my mind, not my body. But this time was different. I was utterly exhausted. I couldn't summon the energy to eat, read, even follow a television program. My sole desire was to sleep most of the day for days at a time.

The strong link between social anxiety and depression may be partly psychological. In many cases, including mine, the anxiety seems to come before the depression. It's easy to see how the constant stress, low self-esteem, negative thinking, and isolation associated with social anxiety could be quite depressing, especially for someone who is already predisposed to mood disorders.

However, there seems to be a physiological link as well. Both social anxiety disorder and depression have been linked to low levels of serotonin in the brain. Some evidence also suggests that both may be associated with low levels of dopamine.

As time went on, the fog of depression that had surrounded me began to lift a bit. I had taken the remainder of the semester off, and gradually I eased back into a more normal routine. I started by simply going upstairs, then going out of the house to grocery shop with my mother. Eventually, I began substitute teaching at my old high school. (I hadn't yet finished my college degree, but that wasn't a requirement to be a substitute teacher.) Unfortunately, I felt as if I had dived back into life much too soon. At every moment, I was terrified that I would say or do something bizarre. After a while, I started declining all offers to teach.

Starving for Approval

The failed trip to Paris had jump-started some problematic eating patterns. When I craved food, I remembered how guilty I felt about the trip, and I used the hunger pangs to punish myself. Hunger also served as a reminder that pretty, skinny girls have friends, and I wanted to be reminded of that all the time.

One year later, I was 60 pounds lighter, having filled every last minute of my junior year at college with work and exercise. In addition to my schoolwork, I had taken on no less than three part-time jobs to ease my guilt over all the money I was costing my parents for the Paris trip, college expenses, and my apartment. I felt a strange sense of satisfaction in the exhaustion and hardship this relentless schedule brought to my life.

The more miserable I was, the more I felt as if I must be achieving something. I bought only bare-bones essentials and made do for everything else. I asked for no creature comforts and even refused repeated offers to transport a bed to my apartment, choosing to sleep on the floor instead.

The tendency toward obsessive thoughts and compulsive behaviors that I had shown as a little girl suddenly came back to haunt me. I saved and catalogued every last recipe that mentioned a particular brand name, although I never cooked. I had neither a TV nor a CD player, and I spent what little free time I had obsessing over cleanliness and routine. I vacuumed twice a day, and I set my table with the same placemat, dishes, and silverware laid in the same order at precisely the same time every morning and evening. I found out later that compulsive behavior often goes hand in hand with an eating disorder.

Though I recognized that I had lost a lot of weight, I didn't see myself as a *real* anorexia sufferer. To me, eating disorders were glamorous conditions exclusive to Hollywood headliners and the spoiled daughters of wealthy families. Me, I was purging in shower stalls, growing chest hair, losing teeth and fingernails, and going bald. It was gross, not glamorous. In my eyes, I was just a girl doing disgusting things in pursuit of an idealized image I would never attain.

Warning Signs of an Eating Disorder

It's not uncommon for people with social anxiety disorder to also have an eating disorder, just as I did. Be alert for these warning signs:

Anorexia nervosa

- Experiencing a sudden, dramatic weight loss
- Refusing to eat or following a very restrictive diet
- Moving your food around on your plate rather than eating it
- Making frequent excuses to avoid mealtimes
- Claiming not to be hungry even when you are
- Counting calories or fat grams obsessively
- Thinking you're too fat when others say you're too thin
- Wearing baggy clothes to hide how much weight you've lost
- Being extremely fearful of gaining weight
- Weighing yourself several times a day
- Thinking and talking about weight and food all the time
- Ceasing menstruation, if you're a female past puberty

Bulimia nervosa

- Eating large amounts of food in a short amount of time
- Forcing yourself to throw up after eating
- Taking laxatives or diuretics to control your weight
- Exercising excessively regardless of weather, illness, or injury
- Showing signs of frequent self-induced vomiting, such as discolored teeth, cuts or calluses on the hands, or swelling of the cheeks or jaw area

Over time, an eating disorder can take a serious toll on your health, leading to malnutrition, heart problems, or even death. If you recognize the danger signs in yourself, it's vital to talk to your doctor or a mental health professional promptly about getting treatment. For further information, please see the eating disorders resources listed in the Resources section at the end of this book.

Spiraling Out of Control

At the end of the term, I moved back into my parents' home. I watched in horror as my belongings, packed and organized so meticulously, were crammed into the damp garage wherever they would fit. My precious privacy was gone. How would I eat? How would I clean? How could I be alone? I felt numb.

I was bursting into tears at the drop of a hat. At one point during the summer, I became so distraught that I refused to get out of the car to walk into a classroom to take an important teaching exam. My thoughts were muddled, and I feared that I wouldn't be able to compose an essay that made any sense. Eventually, my parents gave up trying to persuade me to go inside and turned the car around, driving the hundred miles back to their home with me sobbing in the backseat.

My parents couldn't take it any longer. My father pulled the car alongside a phone booth and telephoned Dr. A. to request an emergency appointment for that afternoon. He was going to drive me straight to Dr. A.'s office.

When I heard the plan, I panicked and screamed at the top of my lungs. I kicked the seats and pounded my fists on the car door. I was *not* going back to a doctor I had stopped seeing over a year ago. I knew I had lost my mind, and I didn't want anyone else to find out. My tantrum proved successful in that my parents canceled the appointment, but I knew I needed help.

I was determined to wait for a "good day"—a day when I felt competent enough to face the doctor without seeming as out of control on the outside as I felt on the inside. Finally, I worked up the courage to ask my mother to make an appointment to get me back on medication. I wanted her to make the call because I still avoided using the telephone.

Finally, I worked up the courage to ask my mother to make an appointment to get me back on medication.

When I saw Dr. A., I didn't mention my temper tantrums, nor did I talk about my extreme eating behavior. To the contrary,

I tried to hide the fact that I was down to 82 pounds by wearing baggy clothes and sporting a short haircut that filled out my face. For one thing, I was afraid it might seem that I was only after attention. Even stronger was the fear that I might reveal the big secret that I was insane. What if I said, "Oh, yes, I throw up while sitting in the bathtub so no one will suspect"? I was sure that was enough to get me sent to an institution, where I would be forced to give up the habits I clung to so desperately.

Soon I would be moving away to student-teach for a semester anyway. As long as I left Dr. A.'s office with a prescription in my hand, I was satisfied. I convinced myself there was no need to divulge all my secrets.

A Big Apple for the Teacher

Weeks later, I was beginning a brand-new student-teaching program for teachers willing to relocate to New York City. Once again, moving hundreds of miles away to a place no one knew me sounded irresistibly appealing.

I made it through the semester, gaining 25 pounds in less than two months by feeding my stress rather than starving it. I binged on packages of sandwich cookies, loaves of Italian bread, and plates of elbow macaroni. Being observed teaching every day and having my daily lesson plans scrutinized by more experienced teachers was horrifying. From August to December of that year, I thought of nothing but school 24 hours a day, 7 days a week.

The depth of my distress is evident in this diary entry from December:

I've heard, and used many times, the expression "bored to death," but it is only now that I comprehend its literal quality. I am so tired of myself and my state and its continual monotonous way that I am dead. Forget suicide. I'm dead. There is no future, no hope for change, no little dreams. This is it. Nothing will make it better; no person can change it. I don't hold out hope. I have no plans to make it dramatic with a note and a noose. There's no point to it.

I don't get excited or depressed. No news could shock me. I saw the best movie of my life last weekend and I silently sobbed to myself because I could make no changes in me—not like the lady in the film. There is no joy, no pit. There just is—

I'd kill for someone to pull me out, but I don't know anyone, and I am so afraid of people that I can't get to know anyone. And who wants to get to know me anyway? I don't even like me. I hate myself.

I've lost all track of time. What happened years ago may as well have happened yesterday. I have no milestones with which to gauge my life. It's not even painful anymore. I'm just numb.

I've just realized a correlation in dreams I've had lately. Last night I dreamed I saved myself from a tornado while my neighbor's roof was blown off. The night before, an anthrax cloud covered the city, but not only did I have a gas mask, I was among the last to get a train out of town. Why do I have dreams of saving myself? Why, if I can do it in my sleep, do I suffer so much awake?

I don't believe anything will bring me back to life.

I left New York once my student-teaching program was completed. I graduated from college one year later, then stayed at school to work on a master's program. However, a few credits short of my master's degree, I decided to return to New York City, accepting a teaching position at a vocational school in the South Bronx. I made up the excuse, at times even convincing myself, that I was doing a valiant deed by going to teach in the inner city. But the truth was, this was just another impulsive decision motivated by a desire to start over. In my mind, choosing a school that was desperate for teachers made it less likely that I would be rejected.

I landed myself in a heap of trouble from the start. The principal asked how soon I could begin working, and fearing they wouldn't want me if they had to wait long, I nervously blurted out "Monday"—a mere five days away. I had less than a week to withdraw from graduate school, move six hundred miles, find a new apartment, and give my current roommate time to find someone to pay half the rent for the apartment we shared.

I found a new apartment in Queens on my second day of work and promptly moved in, only to find that it was infested with cockroaches. I moved back into a hotel and trudged on in my job. A week later, I moved into apartment number two. It wasn't at all glamorous, but at least it was bug-free.

At work, I assumed everyone who laid eyes on me considered me incompetent. Just as in high school, I was the first to arrive in the morning. This time, it was to make photocopies before others could look over my shoulder to ask what lessons I was teaching or imply that I was using too much paper.

My free periods were supposed to be spent making telephone calls to the students' parents, but I couldn't do it. The phone was in a shared office space, and knowing that someone could easily overhear me speaking about my class made it impossible to squeeze the words from my throat. Sometimes I would make my phone calls after school, once everyone had left for the day. In fact, I did much of my work then, because I was too distracted by my concerns about what other people were thinking to plan lessons during work hours. Every evening, I lugged all of my books, files, and papers onto the subway in no less than three giant bags.

I was running myself ragged, waking every morning at 3:30 A.M. after working on schoolwork until midnight the night before. I slept atop a pile of clothes because I lacked a stick of furniture. Late one night, someone broke through the chain lock on my door, and I watched the entire event, beginning to end, with no feeling whatsoever—no fear, no words, no picking up the phone, *nothing*. I merely fixed my eyes on the door and waited. Thankfully, it turned out to be a realtor who thought the apartment was empty and not a rapist who had followed me home.

Three weeks into the job, I walked into my classroom and stared at my students. I couldn't have cared less if a couple of them had decided to throw fists—or bullets—at one another. I wouldn't have minded one bit if someone had smashed the fish tank in front of my desk. Every last one of them could have walked straight out the door, and I wouldn't have said a word. I was a zombie. I no longer felt the person inside of me. I quit that afternoon and never went back.

Emptiness at the Bottom of a Bottle

Never before had I felt so empty. I remember wishing that I could fall into a coma and drop out of the conscious world. On several occasions, I walked to the edge of the platform for the elevated trains that ran though my neighborhood. How easy it would be to lose my balance and slip onto the highway below! The thought of the nuisance it would create for those who might see me fall, run me over, or have to retrieve my body was too exhausting to con-sider.

I found myself staring at nothing for hours on end. At times, I sensed that I was rocking

Go ahead, I thought. Put me in a hospital. No one did.

side to side. *Go ahead*, I thought. *Put me in a hospital.* No one did.

Soon I returned to live with my parents. Then in the spring of 2003, I moved into a 14-by-20-foot storage shed, which I fixed up to be my secluded cabin in the woods. My parents lived a stone's throw down the road, where I went most mornings to shower, eat breakfast, and get ready for the day. The rest of my time was spent in the woods writing stories, gardening, and making items to sell at a local farmers' market. The company I kept was a menagerie of animals from newborn mice to feral cats to a broken-legged pigeon to an old silver mutt I adopted from the pound. Days and nights were spent in complete solitude on 40 acres of woods with no electricity or running water. I had a small wood stove for heat and a battery-operated radio, but subzero January temperatures forced me out in the early days of 2004.

After that, I worked one summer as an assistant theater manager at a local opera house. This job proved to be just another source of agony for me, because it involved using the telephone. I started going to my apartment during lunch hour

---

If You're Abusing Alcohol or Drugs

It's estimated that about 20% of people with social anxiety disorder also have a problem with alcohol or other drugs. If you fall into this group, the National Drug and Alcohol Treatment Referral Routing Service, operated by the federal government's Substance Abuse and Mental Health Services Administration (SAMHSA), has a toll-free number you can call for treatment referrals (800-662-HELP). SAMHSA also provides a searchable online directory of alcohol and drug abuse programs around the country at www.findtreatment.samhsa.gov. For further resources on substance abuse, please see the Resources section at the end of this book.

to drink alcohol in an attempt to make answering the phone less nerve-racking. It did no good, and I ended up more foggy and tired than relaxed. When I began drinking in the morning before work, too, I recognized that it was time to stop.

Fighting for My Life

My job ended, and having no money, I moved back to my parents' house yet again. That fall, I suffered the worst breakdown of my life. I slept most hours of the day, and I wouldn't step outside the front door for weeks at a time. Day after day, I wore the same shirt and jeans, and I obsessed over a strict diet of toast, white sugar, diet cola, vegetable bouillon, and coffee. I began clawing constantly at my skin—first on my hands, but when that became too obvious, I began scratching behind my ears, on my chest, and along my hairline. And as if that weren't unattractive enough, I starting sitting in the bathtub and pulling out my hair in clumps.

Every day I thought about killing myself. I knew it would hurt my parents, but how could I possibly be more of a burden to them than I already was? Day after day, they had to put up with a daughter who did nothing but sleep, sob, and blame everyone from family to society for her situation.

Finally, I made an appointment to see Dr. A., determined to ask for a change in my medication. In the past, I had assumed it would seem presumptuous to request something other than what I had been prescribed. After all, I was no expert. What did I know about psychophar-

By hitting my lowest point, I had found the will to start fighting for my life.

macology? But I was beyond caring about decorum now. By hitting my lowest point, I had found the will to start fighting for my life.

My assumption that it would be inappropriate to ask about a change in medication was completely baseless. In truth, mental health professionals such as Dr. A. *want* patients to play an active role in their own treatment.

Different individuals respond differently to the same medication, and finding the best one at the right dose for a particular person can take some trial and error. As I eventually realized, the more you communicate with your doctor about how you're feeling, any changes you're noticing, and any unwanted side effects you might be experiencing, the easier it is for your doctor to fine-tune your treatment plan.

Be realistic in your expectations. If you're prescribed an antidepressant, as many people with social anxiety disorder are, it can take six to eight weeks to feel the effects. After that time has passed, though, if you still aren't feeling significantly better, talk to your doctor. Depending on the situation, your doctor might sometimes change your dose, add a second medicine, or switch you to a new medication.

New Medication, New Attitude

I arrived at Dr. A.'s office in the same jeans I had been wearing for the past month and sneakers with holes big enough for my socks to show through. For once, I wasn't wearing an uncomfortable smile throughout the whole appointment, but I was still guarded. I shared very little information about my true state of mind, and I never mentioned that I had spent almost all my time in bed for a month. Nevertheless, Dr. A. prescribed a new medication and told me to come back to see him in 30 days.

You don't understand, I thought. *If this doesn't work, I won't be around another two weeks.* As morbid as it sounds, I was convinced that if the new prescription wasn't effective, I would be dead in a matter of days—if not as a result of deliberately harming myself, then as a result of giving up eating and drinking. It was already taking far too much energy to bother fixing myself a cup of bouillon, and I was secretly suffering from chest pain and a heartbeat that felt irregular.

I went home and began taking the new medication. The effect was everything I had hoped for and then some. Before long, I was out of bed and clambering into cupboards, looking for dishes to use for our Thanksgiving meal. Suddenly, I was looking forward to the holidays. I wanted to celebrate with my family, even if I would only be eating toast while everyone else indulged in a feast.

I was fortunate that the medication worked so well, but not every medicine works equally well for every individual. My story might have had a different outcome if this medicine hadn't been the right choice for me. In retrospect, I realize that I took a huge risk by not being more forthcoming with Dr. A. about the true depths of my hopelessness. I won't gamble with my health that way in the future. I certainly hope I never reach the point where I'm thinking about harming myself again, but if I do, I won't just wait around to see what happens. Even though I know it won't be easy, I'll speak up and let a doctor or therapist know how urgently I need help.

Drug Therapy for Social Anxiety Disorder

Medication was a blessing for me, and because it's the treatment I tried first, it's what I'll focus on in this chapter. But keep in mind that psychotherapy, either alone or combined with medication, is an equally important treatment option. (You can learn more about psychotherapy in the next chapter.)

While I began my treatment with medication, many people start with psychotherapy instead. The best researched method of therapy for social anxiety disorder is cognitive-behavioral therapy (CBT), which helps people change destructive thought and behavior patterns that may be contributing to their anxiety. Research has shown that both medication and CBT can be effective for treating social anxiety disorder in young people. Medication may work faster than CBT, but therapy may have more durable effects after treatment is stopped.

Medication may work faster than CBT, but therapy may have more durable effects after treatment is stopped.

For those who don't get enough relief from either medicine or therapy alone, a combination of both may be helpful. In fact, some professionals prefer a combined approach right from the start, on the assumption that two treatments together are stronger than either by itself. While that sounds logical, no studies have yet shown that combination therapy really does lead to better results in adolescents.

Research has found that about 70% of adults who take medication alone for social anxiety disorder get better, compared to just 30% who take a placebo—a sugar pill that looks like the real thing but doesn't contain any active ingredient. There also have been three well-controlled studies in children and teenagers in which treatment with medication showed big advantages over a placebo.

At first, I was surprised to learn that antidepressants—medications used to prevent or relieve depression—are also the most commonly prescribed drugs for social anxiety disorder. But it makes sense when you consider that anxiety and depression involve many of the same changes in brain chemicals. Drugs that target these chemicals often work for either disorder—or for both at once, if you have anxiety and depression at the same time, the way I did.

The dosage and time it takes to feel better may differ for the two conditions, though. It takes six to eight weeks for social anxiety disorder to respond to antidepressants, compared to four to six weeks for depression. In addition, higher doses of some antidepressants may be needed to treat social anxiety disorder than to treat depression.

Selective Serotonin Reuptake Inhibitors (SSRIs)

SSRIs are a group of antidepressants that are widely prescribed for social anxiety disorder. As their name implies, SSRIs block the reuptake, or reabsorption, of serotonin. Here's how the process works: Inside the brain, nerve cells release serotonin into synapses, the tiny spaces between these cells. Later the serotonin is reabsorbed—removed from the synapses and carried back into the nerve cells from which it came. At that point, serotonin is no longer in a position to be helpful. But by interfering with reuptake, SSRIs increase the amount of serotonin left in the synapses, where it's able to be have beneficial effects. SSRIs also may change the number and sensitivity of serotonin receptors within the brain.

A number of studies have shown that SSRIs can be effective against social anxiety disorder in both young people and adults. Two SSRIs, paroxetine (Paxil) and sertraline (Zoloft), are specifically approved by the U.S. Food and Drug Administration (FDA) for the treatment of social anxiety disorder.

Possible side effects of SSRIs include nausea, headaches, nervousness, insomnia, jitteriness, and sexual problems. Most side effects tend to be mild, and they're often temporary. However, some potential side effects are more serious. The FDA has issued a warning about a small but significant risk of increased suicidal thoughts and behaviors in people who take

SSRIs and other antidepressants. Although this warning initially applied only to children and adolescents, in 2005, the FDA began a review that could lead to extending the warning to adults as well. If you have thoughts of suicide, don't wait to see if they go away on their own. Tell your doctor right away.

Serotonin-Norepinephrine Reuptake Inhibitors (SNRIs)

SNRIs are another group of antidepressants that act on serotonin much the way SSRIs do, but that also affect levels of another neurotransmitter called norepinephrine. Like SSRIs, these medications are sometimes prescribed for social anxiety disorder as well as depression. The side effects of SNRIs are similar to those of SSRIs, and the FDA warning about suicidal thoughts and behaviors applies here, too. One SNRI in particular, called venlafaxine (Effexor XR), has been well studied as a social anxiety disorder treatment, and it's approved by the FDA for that use.

Monoamine Oxidase Inhibitors (MAOIs)

MAOIs are yet another class of antidepressants that occasionally are prescribed when other drugs fail. While not FDA approved for this purpose, the MAOI phenelzine (Nardil) has been shown useful for treating social anxiety disorder in controlled trials. The problem is that this class of drugs can cause severe high blood pressure reactions if strict dietary guidelines aren't followed. Due to this risk, many doctors won't prescribe MAOIs. Yet they're the only medications that simultaneously raise serotonin, norepinephrine, and dopamine. As such, they're sometimes helpful for anxiety or depression when other drugs don't work.

Benzodiazepines

Unlike the three previous drug categories, benzodiazepines are not antidepressants. Instead, they're intended specifically to treat anxiety. On the plus side, these medications are quite fast acting. While it can take weeks to feel the full effects of antidepressants, people who take benzodiazepines may feel better almost immediately. Because the pills work so quickly, some people just take them on an as-needed basis. On the minus side, little research has been done on the use of these medications by teenagers, and the results to date have been mixed.

...benzodiazepines are not antidepressants. Instead, they're intended specifically to treat anxiety.

Benzodiazepines can cause side effects such as daytime drowsiness, loss of coordination, fatigue, and decreased mental alertness, which could be a problem at school or work. You might be advised not to drive while taking one of these medications. In addition, combining a benzodiazepine with alcohol can lead to serious or even life-threatening complications, so be honest with your doctor if you drink.

Another drawback to benzodiazepines is that severe withdrawal symptoms can occur if the medication is stopped suddenly after a period of extended use. In fact, you might have some symptoms if you miss just a single dose. Possible signs of withdrawal include anxiety, shakiness, headaches, dizziness, insomnia, and loss of appetite. To minimize the unpleasantness, your doctor can help you taper off your medicine gradually when you're ready to discontinue use.

Buspirone

Buspirone (BuSpar) is in a class by itself. It's the only medication intended specifically for treating anxiety that isn't a benzodiazepine. Unlike benzodiazepines, buspirone must be taken consistently for a couple of weeks to have an effect. In studies with adults, it has been shown to help relieve anxiety, but there isn't enough research to know whether it's equally effective in adolescents. Some doctors still prescribe it for teenagers, though, and there are clinical reports suggesting that it might be helpful for teens who haven't responded to other types of medication.

Tips on Taking Your Medicine

Over the years, I've taken a few different medications, including two SSRIs and buspirone, and I've learned some strategies for getting the most out of them. First of all, be sure to tell your doctor about any other prescription medications, nonprescription medicines, or herbal supplements you're taking. Some of these substances can interact harmfully with each other. For example, mixing an SSRI or SNRI with certain migraine medicines called triptans can lead to a dangerous serotonin syndrome—an adverse drug reaction in which there is too much serotonin in the brain. Symptoms include restlessness, hallucinations, loss of coordination, fast heart beat, increased body temperature, fast changes in blood pressure, overactive reflexes, diarrhea, nausea, vomiting, and coma. By informing your doctor about any other medicines you're taking, you can help guard against this type of problem.

Don't stop your medication without talking to your doctor first.

Don't stop your medication without talking to your doctor first. It's tempting to stop as soon as you're feeling better, but remember that the medicine may be the reason you're feeling that way. If you and your doctor decide that it's time to discontinue a medication, gradual withdrawal is often advisable.

If you have trouble remembering your medicine, try marking off each time you take it on a calendar that you post in a prominent spot. You might also want to buy a weekly pillbox, which has a separate compartment for each day's pills. That way, it's easy to tell whether you've taken your medicine or not.

Finally, don't expect a miracle. While medication can help relieve symptoms, it won't necessarily erase all your fears and worries overnight. That's where psychotherapy can be helpful, by addressing the psychological side of the disorder the same way medication addresses the physiological side.

The Next Fork in the Road

Within a few weeks of starting my latest medicine, I had set my sights on finding a job. But after several failed attempts, such as my failure to show up on the first day to train as a restaurant hostess, Dr. A. suggested that I consider applying for disability coverage. I resisted. In the back of my mind, I still believed that I could fight and win. I was determined to try everything before accepting that I was unemployable.

I approached my parents with the idea that I go somewhere, anywhere, to get psychotherapy for social anxiety disorder. They were pleased that I was motivated, and they tended to support me when I was at my most optimistic. Yet I sensed that they were skeptical.

That afternoon, I sat down at the computer and began researching intensive treatment programs for social anxiety disorder. I made a fateful hit on my first try. I had been connected to The Ross Center for Anxiety & Related Disorders in Washington, DC. The center was directed by Jerilyn Ross, M.A.,

Medications for Social Anxiety Disorder

In the chart below, medications marked with an asterisk (*) have been specifically approved by the FDA for the treatment of social anxiety disorder.

Category of drug	Specific medications	How they may work
Selective serotonin reuptake inhibitors	citalopram (Celexa) escitalopram (Lexapro) fluoxetine (Prozac) fluvoxamine (Luvox) paroxetine (Paxil)* sertraline (Zoloft)*	Increase the concentration and activity of serotonin
Serotonin-norepinephrine reuptake inhibitors	duloxetine (Cymbalta), venlafaxine (Effexor XR)*	Increase serotonin activity and also affect norepinephrine
Monoamine oxidase inhibitors	isocarboxazid (Marplan) phenelzine (Nardil) tranylcypromine (Parnate)	Increase serotonin, norepinephrine, and dopamine levels
Benzodiazepines	alprazolam (Xanax) chlordiazepoxide (Librium) clonazepam (Klonopin) clorazepate (Tranxene) diazepam (Valium) lorazepam (Ativan) oxazepam (Serax)	May enhance levels of gamma-amino-butyric acid (GABA)
Other antianxiety medication	buspirone (BuSpar)	Increases serotonin activity

LIC.S.W., the president and CEO of the Anxiety Disorders Association of America. Hers was the book I had relished in the secluded corners of the library during my freshman year of college. I filled out an online application and hit the "submit" key.

A week later, I was shocked to hear Jerilyn Ross herself on the other end of the telephone inviting me to Washington for five days of outpatient therapy. I had suddenly joined the ranks of the lucky ones.

Chapter Six

Five Days That Changed My Life

The money I was costing my parents had been steadily adding up. By the spring of 2005, I had drained tens of thousands of dollars from their bank accounts by pursuing failed stays in faraway places and start-up businesses that would have allowed me to work completely by myself, but that never seemed to get off the ground. My medical insurance covered none of the cost of monthly visits to the psychiatrist or the medication I was taking, so my parents paid for those, too. They had also financed my undergraduate degree as well as the graduate degree that I hadn't finished, and they had paid the security deposits and monthly rent for no fewer than five apartments. The cost was straining my relationship not only with my parents, but also with my sisters, who implied that my constant financial demands were extremely selfish.

To my family, an intensive treatment program in Washington, DC, complete with train fare and a week's worth of hotel accommodations, must have seemed like the latest in a long line of expensive nonsolutions. To me, though, this plan felt different. This time, I was confronting my anxiety, not running from it. The treatment I had read about, *dreamed* about—the treatment that I thought was only for the lucky, rich, or well connected—was suddenly available to me. I had neither money of my own nor highly placed friends, but I was determined, and it was determination that set everything in motion.

It took courage to address my anxiety with the seriousness it deserved. In the past, I had made fun of myself and laughed off my problems, but now I was forced to admit to my parents that anxiety was affecting my life to a sobering degree. Bravery in this context meant being completely honest with them, knowing full well that they might view the trip as just another selfish scheme that was probably doomed to failure. Mustering the confidence to counter their skepticism wasn't easy for me. It was tempting to call everything off, but that would have gotten me nowhere.

> It took courage to address my anxiety with the seriousness it deserved.

Adding to my trepidation was the knowledge that, once I began five days of intensive treatment in Washington, I would be asked to do the very things I had so long avoided. I would be expected to go into stores and restaurants, ask for help at service counters, maybe even talk on the telephone. To make the most of this opportunity, I also would need to put myself on the line and be totally candid with the therapist.

Getting Intense in Washington

Despite my reservations, I was more optimistic about trying this treatment program than I had been about anything else for a long time, and my eagerness soon won over my parents. Before long, I found myself at the treatment center in Washington.

I was assigned to Dr. Q. for treatment. From day one, I felt comfortable sharing my experiences with her. Dr. Q. seemed at ease, too, as she listened attentively to everything I said. I can't say for sure whether or not she felt as though we clicked, but something definitely clicked inside me.

I was as forthright as I had ever been about my history, speaking as openly as I could about my troubled relationships, failed jobs, and alienation from my family. Dr. Q. showed nothing but interest—no alarm, no annoyance. It felt incredibly good to finally release so many thoughts that I had kept pent up for years, afraid that I would come across as too needy or selfish. After talking with Dr. Q., I felt lighter and more enthusiastic than ever about making another new beginning. This time, I believed, the changes were finally going to stick.

The cornerstone of my treatment with Dr. Q. was cognitive-behavioral therapy (CBT). The cognitive part of CBT involved looking at my automatic thoughts (for example, "They'll think I'm crazy") and learning how to challenge those thoughts as a way of lowering my anxiety. The behavioral part involved noticing my counterproductive behaviors (for example, avoiding the phone) and finding more helpful ways of dealing with situations that made me anxious.

As I examined my own thinking, it soon became clear that I assumed everyone who came into contact with me immediately conjured a negative image of the type of person I was. I read it in their faces, their body language, and the tone of their voices, and I considered myself an expert at gauging other people's impressions.

"So you're a mind reader," Dr. Q. said. I wanted to say yes, but that might have sounded presumptuous.

Then Dr. Q. posed a question: What would a waitress think if I dropped my fork at a restaurant and asked for a replacement. I had no doubt that the waitress would be annoyed, thinking that I was demanding and rude. I haltingly tried to express this thought to Dr. Q., choosing my words carefully. But I had trouble getting the thought out because I kept mentally backtracking, worrying about how Dr. Q. would perceive my words.

"Where's your evidence that she thinks you're annoying?" Dr. Q. asked.

"She might take a deep breath," I suggested, "or be overly friendly about getting a fork for me, when really she wants to strangle me."

"Assume she does take a deep breath. What are a few reasons for her doing that?"

I gave the answer that I thought Dr. Q. wanted to hear. "She might be having a bad day."

"Or . . . ," Dr. Q. prompted.

"She might be tired."

"Or . . ."

I thought some more. "She might really be annoyed at me."

"Or . . ."

"She might not be sighing at all."

"Do you know what she's thinking?" Dr. Q. asked.

"No."

"So are you a mind reader? Tell me," Dr. Q. continued, "what are the job requirements for a waitress?"

"To serve food."

"And . . ."

"To help customers if they drop a fork," I said, smiling.

"Do you think you'd have been the only person to ask for another fork or cup or spoon?" Dr. Q. asked. "Don't you think she expects it as part of her job?"

My first summer out of high school, I had worked briefly as a waitress (not the best job for a person who becomes anxious around strangers, I quickly discovered after many forgotten orders and dropped trays). On numerous occasions, I was asked for everything from forks to extra plates to free meals, and never had I judged a customer based on this kind of request. Dr. Q. was right. I *wasn't* a mind reader, although objectively assessing the possible explanations for other people's behavior was something that wouldn't come easily for a long time.

CBT for Social Anxiety Disorder

Psychotherapy is the formal name for therapy that uses psychological and behavioral methods to treat mental and emotional disorders. CBT is a particular form of psychotherapy that helps people recognize and change self-defeating thought patterns as well as identify and change maladaptive behaviors. It's the best-researched type of psychotherapy for treating social anxiety disorder. Several randomized, controlled clinical trials—the gold standard for clinical research—have found that CBT is effective at reducing social anxiety in young people as well as adults.

Thoughts, Behaviors, and Anxiety

After reading this far, you've undoubtedly seen how thoughts and behaviors can intensify and perpetuate social anxiety. Let's say you are convinced that everyone in your class finds you dumb and boring. When called upon to answer a question in class, the first thought that pops into your mind might be something like, *Oh, no! I'm going to say something stupid*—even when you actually know the material quite well. The next thought that follows is apt to be something like, *They're going to think I'm a fool*, or, *Everybody is going to laugh at me*.

Of course, some negative thoughts are perfectly rational. If you haven't paid attention in class or cracked a book all semester, it's reasonable to worry about how you're going to do on an upcoming test. Such thoughts serve a useful purpose by alerting you to potential problems and perhaps motivating you to take preventive action. The trouble arises when you get into the habit of *irrational* negative thinking, such as expecting to give the wrong answer when you know the right one or assuming that other people are focused on judging you all the time.

Everyone has unrealistic thoughts now and then. However, for people with social anxiety disorder, unrealistic thoughts about embarrassing yourself or being judged harshly become a deeply ingrained habit. After a while, such thoughts may pop into your mind so quickly and automatically that you barely notice them, but you *do* notice the sudden self-consciousness that results. This self-consciousness, in turn, can lead to counterproductive behavior. When called on in class, for example, you might forget an answer that you know or mumble the answer incoherently.

At this point, you've created a self-fulfilling prophecy in which your thoughts and behaviors have conspired to ensure that your initial fear was realized. Now let's say you replay the scene over and over in your mind at home that night, berating yourself each time for your "stupidity." The next day, the thought of facing your classmates—all of whom, you're sure, will be snickering to themselves over your humiliation—is apt to send your anxiety level shooting through the roof.

This heightened anxiety just makes it all the more difficult to calm your nerves and respond appropriately the next time you're called on in class, and that, in turn, only makes the anxiety worse. It's easy to see how destructive this type of cycle could be. The goal of CBT is to break the chain of self-defeating thoughts

The goal of CBT is to break the chain of self-defeating thoughts and behaviors...

and behaviors so that you can replace them with more constructive responses.

The cognitive part of CBT involves taking note of your thoughts in various situations. The therapist then helps you learn to evaluate how realistic the thoughts truly are. At times, the therapist may challenge you to put your thinking to the real-world test. At other times, you might be asked to consider whether the worst-case outcome really would be as disastrous as you've imagined. Once you've identified thinking patterns that don't stand up to the reality test, your therapist will guide you through the process of substituting more constructive thoughts.

Taking Therapy Beyond the Office

Where's my evidence?, and, *Am I mind reading?* were questions that remained with me as I carried out my afternoon assignments. I was sent to ask for travel books at a bookstore and directions to a nearby library. I also was supposed to go sightseeing, which gave me another chance to try out some of my new ways of thinking.

The other part of my assignment was to chart my anxiety on a scale from one (lowest) to ten (highest) before, during, and after each activity. Beside each number, I was to record my physical symptoms, such as a racing heart, dry mouth, chattering teeth, yawning, or blushing. I also recorded my thoughts, from which I discovered that the anticipation of an event was often far more anxiety provoking than the event itself.

"Go do your assignments," said Dr. Q., tapping her notes into a neat stack, "and tomorrow we'll go for lunch."

Lunch? I hadn't eaten in public in years. Yet I just smiled, nodded, and agreed with a high-pitched "okay." After fumbling with the door, I set out to complete an afternoon's worth of assigned tasks.

Assignment: Asking for travel books
Anxiety level: 8
Physical symptoms: Chattering teeth, tightness in chest, feeling of "tuning out"
Thoughts: They're going to think I'm lazy for not finding the books myself and be annoyed with me. I won't get my words out, which will only make me stand out all the more. I'm going to come across as an annoying tourist.
Am I mind-reading? Yes
Rethinking: Part of a bookstore clerk's job is to help customers find books. The store has numerous customers everyday. My request is quite ordinary.

The store was bustling with weekend shoppers. Right before my eyes was the display of travel books. How could I possibly ask for assistance when the section was directly in front of me? *They're going to be annoyed*, I thought. *They'll think I'm the stupidest, laziest person alive!* As I wandered around the store, exaggerated thoughts such as these filled my head. They'd think I was nuts if I asked for help! I left the store, intending to return the next morning before my therapy appointment.

Assignment: Asking directions to the library at the Metro booth
Anxiety level: 7
Physical symptoms: Tightness in chest, dry mouth, butterflies
Thoughts: They'll laugh at me for being nerdy and seeking out a library. They'll be annoyed because their job doesn't entail directing girls to libraries.
Am I mind reading? Yes
Rethinking: If the roles were reversed, I wouldn't mind if someone asked.

I worked up my courage and approached an employee to ask for directions. The response was, "I don't know," but I still felt victorious. I hadn't stumbled over my words, and the reply hadn't sent me into a fit of tears. My anxiety level dropped to a 6 during the exchange, and by the time I walked away, it was a mere 5.

For the sightseeing part of my assignment, I went to the National Gallery of Art. Walking through the gallery, I stayed alert for my old thinking habits. Each time I caught myself assuming that other people thought I was ugly, out of place, and annoying, I asked myself, *Where's my evidence?* It sounds so simple, but I found that this change in mindset really did help me feel less exposed in public.

How Exposure Therapy Works

One key element of CBT for social anxiety disorder is exposure therapy, which involves systematically confronting the situations that frighten you, working up from less threatening situations to more threatening ones. The underlying premise is that the best way to overcome an irrational fear is by facing it head on. You begin with tasks that involve little risk of rejection or disapproval, such as my first few assignments. Later you move on to higher-stakes tasks, but only after you've developed the emotional skills to cope with any negative reaction you might encounter. As positive experiences mount, you stop expecting the worst all the time and start having more confidence in your ability to handle social situations, come what may. Over time, your social anxiety naturally begins to fade away.

As positive experiences mount, you stop expecting the worst all the time...

Typically, the first step in exposure therapy is to develop a list of situations in which you experience social anxiety. Once you have a preliminary list, you and your therapist may work to refine it, teasing out the specific components that make a situation more or less threatening. For example, let's say one thing that makes you anxious is striking up a conversation with a classmate. While this might be true in general, factors such as the gender or familiarity of the classmate might affect exactly how anxious you feel in a particular situation. So one item on your list might be talking to a longtime acquaintance of the same sex, and another might be talking to a classmate of the opposite sex for the first time.

Next you rate each item according to how much anxiety it causes and how likely you would be to try avoiding the situation if it actually came up. The ratings allow you to rank the items on your list from least anxiety-provoking to most. At this point, you're ready to begin confronting the situations you fear, gradually progressing from the easiest tasks to the most difficult.

There are several ways to practice facing your fears. You might start by talking about a scary situation or imagining yourself in it. Next you might role-play the anxiety-provoking scenario in therapy. A high-tech alternative that's currently being investigated is virtual reality exposure therapy, which delivers imagery and sound through a special helmet to create the illusion of actually being inside a computer-generated scene. This allows you to practice facing a feared situation without actually being there. For example, giving a practice speech in front of a virtual audience simulates the experience of public speaking. Finally, you expose yourself to the actual situation in the real world.

Therapy for social anxiety disorder can take place either one-on-one with a therapist or in a small group that's led by

---

Other Behavioral Techniques

Exposure therapy is one important component of CBT for social anxiety disorder, but other techniques often are incorporated as well. When these approaches are combined with exposure therapy, they may add to the benefits:

- *Social skills training* helps you learn specific behaviors through practice and rehearsal that can be applied to various social situations. For example, you might practice looking people in the eye when talking to them.
- *Relaxation training* helps you learn how to calm your mind and relax your body in situations that lead to anxiety and stress. Examples of relaxation techniques include breathing exercises, imagery, and meditation.

---

a therapist and composed of other people with similar anxiety problems. Having at least some of your sessions in group therapy allows you to practice your social skills in a safe environment before venturing out into less predictable settings. The group interaction gives you a chance to find out whether your behavior is really as hopeless as you think it is, whether

Having at least some of your sessions in group therapy allows you to practice your social skills in a safe environment...

other people are actually going to judge you negatively, and how much it matters even if they do. Armed with what you have learned, you'll be better prepared to face your fears—and ultimately overcome them—in real-life situations.

Confronting My Fears Head-On

On the second day of my treatment with Dr. Q., the two of us went to a restaurant for lunch as planned. I used the occasion to confide in Dr. Q. that toast was the only solid food I had eaten for the last five months.

"Even in Washington?" she asked.

"I packed it," I replied.

Dr. Q. was less impressed with my 150 straight days of toast than I was. She seemed more concerned about the adverse effect that my severely restricted diet might be having on the effectiveness of my medication. As we sat in the restaurant, she with her lunch and I with my coffee, she recommended that I get a particular book about maximizing the potential of antidepressants through diet. It was a good excuse for going back to the bookstore.

After lunch, I returned to the store and bought the book, then spent the afternoon reading it in the store's café. The book explained how I could reprogram my diet and exercise habits to make myself feel healthier and more energized. That evening, I threw away my supply of bread.

The next morning, I went out to breakfast for the first time in years. I had never tasted such delicious blueberry yogurt in all my life. Later that day, I was reading sections of my journal aloud to Dr. Q.—an embarrassing but useful substitute for conversation, which still made me extremely self-conscious. When I got to the part about breakfast, a smile came over Dr. Q. 's face. I had done something "huge" (her word) with no prompting. It was a tangible sign of my progress, and I proudly continued to eat in restaurants for the remainder of the trip.

That same day, Dr. Q. and I went to a meeting of Toastmasters International, a club that helps its members develop public-speaking skills. Dr. Q. sat beside me at the meeting, periodically leaning over to ask about my anxiety level or writing me notes as club members gave their speeches. I was invited to the podium to give an impromptu speech, but I declined. Dr. Q., on the other hand, accepted her invitation. As I watched her speak, knowing it was done for my benefit, I was filled with fresh appreciation.

Heading back to the office, Dr. Q. asked what I would have said about myself if I had chosen to address the group. My mind went blank. I desperately tried to pull my thoughts together, but much to my embarrassment, all that came out was a disjointed and tearful monologue. By the time Dr. Q. dropped me off, I felt as though I had made a horrendous fool of myself. I envisioned Dr. Q. driving away in her car, thinking what an annoying and foolish patient I was.

Then I caught myself. This seemed like a perfect time to apply some of the CBT strategies I had just learned. *Am I mind reading?* I asked myself. *Where's my evidence Dr. Q. thinks I'm annoying? What are some alternate possibilities for what she might be thinking? Could she possibly be pleased with my efforts?* I still needed practice, but I was starting to get the hang of analyzing and reframing my thoughts.

Surviving the "End of the World"

On morning number four, I was asked to introduce myself at a staff meeting at the treatment center. Jerilyn Ross would be there along with other staff members. Thoughts of what a fool I had made of myself the previous evening were reason enough to make my immediate response a flat "no." I would rather have given eight impromptu speeches at Toastmasters than introduce myself to the author of the book I had read day after day as a college freshman.

Nevertheless, after a little prodding, I reluctantly agreed. I reminded myself that I had three days of progress behind me. The new strategies I had learned were designed to carry me through just this type of uncomfortable situation. As long as

I stayed alert for overly negative thinking, I couldn't go wrong—could I?

As soon as I entered the office, I was struck speechless. Questions from staff members echoed in my ears. The more I tried to concentrate on what I was being asked, the less sense their words seemed to make. My eyes filled with tears as I found myself unable to formulate coherent answers.

I wanted nothing more than to get out of there, but no group of anxiety experts was about to excuse me at the height of my discomfort. To leave at that point would only strengthen my belief that I was incapable of facing a roomful of people. On the other hand, if I were to stay and work through my anxiety, I'd learn that the 10 I was experiencing could eventually go down to an 8 and possibly even a 6.

I realized that I would have to work through the humiliation I was feeling as I tearfully struggled to come up with words. The staff members suggested relaxation strategies (such as letting myself go "like a rag doll") and conversation starters (such as asking each person in turn whether he or she had any children). After what seemed like a lifetime, I was finally excused.

In the safety of Dr. Q.'s office, I sobbed without restraint. These weren't the dainty tears I had been dabbing away with the corners of folded tissues. These were very real, very hard sobs that I had to let my guard down to cry. I felt embarrassed, broken, and defeated, but at the same time, I felt some relief. I was finally expressing my true feelings in front of someone.

"Don't go back and spend the rest of the day in your hotel room," warned Dr. Q.

I took her advice and went to a restaurant instead. At the lunch counter, I forced myself to recollect everything about the meeting and write it in my journal. I refused to ignore it, push it away, or pretend it had never happened. The more

I wrote, the more perspective I gained. What happened wasn't pleasant, but it wasn't the end of the world, either. I could learn from the experience and be better prepared

What happened wasn't pleasant, but it wasn't the end of the world, either.

the next time I was faced with a similar situation.

Finding Your Own Dr. Q.

I was lucky enough to receive my first taste of CBT at a well-known, highly regarded treatment center, but there are excellent cognitive-behavioral therapists across the country. Therapists with specific training and experience in using exposure therapy to treat social anxiety disorder are harder to find, however. Good starting places include the Anxiety Disorders Association of America (www.adaa.org) and the Association for Behavioral and Cognitive Therapies (www.abct.org), both of which offer searchable directories of treatment providers on their Web sites.

These are some questions you might want to ask when choosing a therapist:

- What type of licensure and credentials do you have?
- How much experience do you have with CBT, especially exposure therapy?
- Will you or a staff member make home visits to do exposures if necessary?
- How many of your patients have social anxiety disorder?
- How many of your patients are teenagers or young adults?
- Do you offer individual therapy, group therapy, or both?
- How often will we meet, and how long will each session last?

- How many sessions do you estimate will be required?
- Can you prescribe medication? If not, are you willing to work with someone who can, if medication is needed?
- Where are you located, and what are your office hours?
- What are your fees? Do you offer reduced fees for people with no insurance and limited financial resources?
- What types of insurance plans do you accept?

The role of a therapist isn't to be a friend, but it certainly helps if you can establish a comfortable rapport the way I did with Dr. Q. When something is making you uncomfortable, it's best to talk about the issue openly, even though that may be difficult. If the problem persists, or if you feel that your concerns aren't being taken seriously, you might want to seek a second opinion. However, it's generally better to work out the problem with your own therapist if you can.

Paying for Mental Health Care

Finding a good therapist is one thing. Paying for the treatment is quite another. Even if you have health insurance, be aware that coverage for mental health care often isn't as extensive as it is for other medical services. Call your insurance plan representative to find out exactly what's covered and what isn't. If only part of the cost is covered, find out how much you'll have to pay out of your own pocket. Also ask about limits on the number of visits, and annual or lifetime maximums.

Educate yourself about how your insurance plan works *before* an urgent situation comes up. Some plans require that you choose from a network of approved providers. In addition, most plans will only cover services that satisfy the standard for "medical necessity," which means the services are deemed medically appropriate and necessary to meet a patient's health care needs. If you're ever denied coverage based on this standard for a service that your provider thinks you need, ask your insurance company about the procedure to appeal the decision.

If you don't have private insurance, you still might qualify for coverage through Medicaid or the State Child Health Insurance Program (SCHIP), two government programs that provide medical and mental health care to those who meet eligibility criteria. Medicaid provides health insurance to eligible low-income and disabled individuals, while SCHIP provides health insurance for the children in certain lower-income families who aren't eligible for Medicaid. Program specifics vary from state to state. To find out exactly what your state offers, start with GovBenefits.gov (800-333-4636, www.govbenefits.gov). If you're 18 or younger, also check out Insure Kids Now! (877-543-7669, www.insurekidsnow.gov).

Unfortunately, many people are caught in a gray area. They don't have adequate coverage under private insurance, but they also don't qualify for government programs. If that's your situation, ask whether your treatment provider offers reduced fees or a payment plan. Community mental health centers are another option. These facilities provide a wide range of mental health services regardless of ability to pay. Fees are set on a sliding scale based on your or your parents' income and the cost of services.

Finally, if you have the opportunity, you might want to consider participating in a research project that's studying treatments for social anxiety disorder. By volunteering to take part, you may gain access to high-quality care for free. You'll be fully informed about the potential risks and benefits before you sign up. If you're a minor, your parent or guardian will be required to give their consent. The Anxiety Disorders Association of America lists some clinical trials that are currently seeking participants on its Web site (www.adaa.org/gettinghelp/ClinicalTrials.asp).

Making the Most of Psychotherapy

In addition to the skill and experience of the therapist, the mental readiness and ability of the person in therapy have a strong effect on the outcome. CBT isn't something that's done for you. It's something you do for yourself under the guidance of a therapist. The more you put into it, the more you'll get back out.

Exposure therapy, in particular, requires a major commitment. It takes great courage to force yourself to face your fears. At first, you may have a short-term increase in anxiety and distress, and you might be tempted to

> It takes great courage to force yourself to face your fears.

give up at that point. If you can push past the initial discomfort, though, you may be pleasantly surprised by the progress you make. For me, the desire for relief was enough to get me through the unpleasant parts, and I can vouch that my efforts were amply repaid.

Homework assignments are often an integral part of CBT. Such assignments let you practice and strengthen the skills you've learned in therapy until they start to feel like second nature. Just as with school homework, it's easy to get lazy and slack off. If you do, though, you'll only be shortchanging yourself. For the best possible results in the least possible time, it's important to give therapy all you've got.

If you have trouble completing an assignment, be honest with your therapist. This can be harder than it sounds for someone with social anxiety disorder, since you may fear that the therapist will think badly of you. Just keep in mind that your therapist is there to help you, not to judge you. You and your therapist can work together to fine-tune the assignments. For example, you might decide to break down an especially difficult task into three or four more manageable chunks. The two of you also can explore ways to anticipate and handle obstacles that may arise. For example, you might talk about ways to keep up your practice while you're on vacation.

If your treatment provider recommends combining therapy with medication, you should probably take that advice to heart. CBT has some definite benefits. Numerous studies have shown that it's effective against social anxiety disorder, and it doesn't carry the same risk of side effects as medication. CBT also teaches you valuable skills that you can use for the rest of your life.

On the other hand, medication directly addresses the imbalance in brain chemicals that underlies the disorder. Some studies have found that medication works faster, while the effects of CBT are more durable. However, other studies have found that the two treatments are roughly equivalent. For some people, a combination of both may be the best treatment choice.

Like medication, therapy takes some time to work. During the first session or two, you and your therapist will decide on the goals you want to accomplish. After a few sessions, you should feel as if you're making some progress toward those

---

An Antianxiety Antibiotic?

Wouldn't it be great if there were a pill that could help you learn more from therapy? Recent research suggests that D-cycloserine, an antibiotic used to treat tuberculosis, might do just that. Previous studies had shown that D-cycloserine stimulates learning in both animals and humans. In a study led by researchers at Boston University, 27 adults with social anxiety disorder were randomly assigned to receive either D-cycloserine or a placebo—a sugar pill that looks like the real thing, but that doesn't contain any active ingredient. The participants took a pill one hour before each of four exposure therapy sessions that focused on the fear of public speaking.

During the sessions, participants gave speeches in front of a video camera or other group members, then listened to feedback. Social anxiety was assessed before treatment, after treatment, and a month after the final session. Participants who received D-cycloserine before their exposure therapy reported less anxiety than those who got a placebo. One advantage to this approach is that it requires just a few doses of medication, which reduces the risk of adverse side effects. By speeding up learning, it might decrease the number of therapy sessions needed as well. These results still need to be confirmed by more research, but they appear very promising.

goals. Don't hesitate to talk it over with your therapist if you ever feel stalled. Even if all seems to be moving along well, the two of you should still review your progress periodically.

Realistically, there may be outside factors that influence how long you stay in therapy, such as the number of sessions your insurance plan will cover. As much as possible, though, the decision about how long to continue therapy should be based on when you successfully achieve your primary goals. If you're still short of your goals but feeling discouraged or thinking about quitting, let your therapist know. Such feelings and thoughts are very common, and they may even be a positive sign, because they're often an outgrowth of moving on to harder challenges. I can't tell you that therapy is an easy process, but I *can* tell you that sticking with it is the best decision I ever made.

Five Days Down, the Rest of My Life to Go

On the fifth and final day of my intensive treatment, I announced a major change I planned to make in my life: I was going back to school to finish my master's degree that summer. Dr. Q. stunned me by asking if I would consider teaching in Washington the following fall so that we could continue working together. In the meantime, Dr. Q. and I would have telephone sessions—something I would have considered impossible before, given my fear and avoidance of using the phone. I was ecstatic, for I had convinced myself that Dr. Q. would be relieved once I was gone.

"One more thing," she said. "Jerilyn Ross wants to talk to you before you go."

I had one more day to push myself, so I agreed. Seven years after reading the stories that got me through my freshman year of college, I finally had the opportunity to thank Jerilyn Ross for the hope she had given me. Although my words weren't as eloquent as I would have liked, I made my gratitude known.

Then she said something I'll never forget: "What you did yesterday was like someone who's afraid of heights dangling from a helicopter." She went to her desk and wrote me a note that I carry in my wallet to this day. It reads:

Emily,
Thank you for being so brave and strong. Remember you can do anything you can't.
Best,
Jerilyn

We exchanged a hug, and I left.

Back home again, I missed the Ross Center, where people such as Jerilyn Ross and Dr. Q. neither defined me by my nervous habits nor let me off the hook when I wanted to walk away from frightening or embarrassing situations. At the treatment center, I was recognized for doing ordinary things that most people do without a second thought, but that, for me, took great determination and courage. Now I was faced with getting through the remainder of the spring and summer on my own. I would continue using the strategies Dr. Q. had taught me, but I wouldn't have her close by for face-to-face support, so it was a bittersweet graduation.

Yet I knew I would never go back to the way things had been before. I had come too far and gained too much hope for the future.

Chapter Seven

Making Changes and Sticking to Them

I returned home from my week at the Ross Center determined to face the situations I had grown accustomed to avoiding in the past. For the first time in years, I felt confident that I was moving in the right direction, and I pushed myself to keep up the momentum. I seized every opportunity to run errands, eat at restaurants, and answer the phone. My local chapter of Toastmasters International met once a week, and I signed up to work on speaking off the cuff.

Daunting tasks such as these were made a little easier by the knowledge that I would be in touch on a regular basis with Dr. Q. Since I had left Washington, we were no longer able to meet in person, but we still spoke by phone every ten days. I knew I could count on Dr. Q. to congratulate my efforts, offer advice, and encourage me to push myself even harder when I was ready.

Still, five days of treatment hadn't erased all my discomfort over speaking about my feelings at length, especially on the phone. To smooth the way for my phone sessions with Dr. Q., I would e-mail her a few days prior to each call, updating her on how I was doing. The e-mails provided topics for our later phone conversations. They revealed that, at times, I continued to struggle when it came to connecting with people. At other times, though, I was making significant progress by altering my thinking patterns, expanding my diet, and registering for summer courses.

> The confidence I gained by facing smaller challenges strengthened my belief that I could succeed...

Some changes came more easily than others. Gradually, however, I began overcoming old habits by questioning evidence and asking myself whether I was mind reading. The confidence I gained by facing smaller challenges strengthened my belief that I could succeed at managing more difficult situations, too.

Mastering My Master's Degree

In May of 2005, I returned to school to finish my master's degree in education. It was a challenge taking the first steps, such as contacting the graduate office and requesting the necessary paperwork. After that, I faced the hurdle of making arrangements over the telephone for a place to stay. Once those hurdles had been cleared, however, it was relatively easy to fall into the routine of classes. Offering ideas while working in small groups wasn't as difficult as it had been in the past, and small talk during class breaks wasn't the torture I remembered it to be.

Yet my anxiety hadn't completely disappeared. Although I had hoped it wouldn't, my throat still clenched up when I was called on to give answers in front of the class. In fact, I volunteered answers so rarely that one professor who never called on students eventually demanded that everyone in the class give a response to the stories we were reading. When I still didn't speak up, she flatly asked, "Emily, what did you think of this passage?" I read a few comments from my notes so I wouldn't have to speak off the top of my head. I still doubted my ability to speak well enough to make any sense.

That same professor suggested holding class at her home, where our group of ten students could cook a noon meal and discuss our weekly papers over lunch. I was concerned that I wouldn't be able to handle a knife or hot skillet in front of my classmates. I also was still selective about my diet, and under ordinary circumstances, I never so much as tasted a crumb in front of other people. But I took the unusual class setting as one more challenge, and I vowed to push myself further each time we met.

At first, I felt out of place as my classmates chatted effortlessly about favorite authors and restaurants. There were days when I walked home from class in tears, but I was determined to stick it out. I set goals for myself, such as initiating a topic of discussion at least once during the three-hour class. At the next meeting, I might set a goal of volunteering at least two answers. As the weeks passed, I began to ease my way into the course.

For example, initially, I simply smiled and quietly offered to stir whatever was on the stove while my classmates chatted. Later, I would make myself ask about everyone's pets or their families. To give another example, early on, I jumped at the opportunity to set the table in the other room. Later, I would share the task with a few other classmates and make a point of joining in the conversation as we moved the chairs. Some days, I was so proud of my efforts that I couldn't wait to relate my progress to Dr. Q.

In the ideal ending to this story, I would finish the class as the most popular student and teacher's pet. I didn't. In fact, my old, perfectionistic self might have seen the experience as a failure. After all, I didn't make any close friends among my classmates, I didn't taste much of what we cooked, and there were days when I barely spoke at all. Yet there were little triumphs, too. I managed small talk when I was among the first to arrive at the teacher's house. I spoke up when it was hard to do. And by the final month, I had enough nerve to attend private meetings with the professor to discuss a major project. Perhaps

Giving myself credit when credit was due was one of my proudest achievements.

most importantly, I recognized when I showed improvement. Giving myself credit when credit was due was one of my proudest achievements.

Coping With Social Anxiety at School

Whether as a student or as a teacher, much of my life—and much of my social anxiety—has revolved around school. I can't say that I ever completely vanquished my fear of being judged in school situations, but I did manage to subdue my anxiety enough to finish my master's degree. To me, that was a major victory.

Below are some common challenges faced by students with social anxiety disorder, along with coping suggestions. The pointers are based not only on my personal experiences, but also on the advice of experts. Because everyone is different, some of these situations may be much more difficult for you than others, and some of the suggestions may be more appropriate for your situation. Think of these ideas as a starting point, not the final word on how to handle your anxiety.

Talking in Class

For me, speaking up in class was among my biggest fears. As I later found out, it's a common fear for other students with social anxiety disorder, too. One study, published in the

Journal of the American Academy of Child and Adolescent Psychiatry, included 50 children and young teenagers with social anxiety. When these children were asked about what caused them distress, almost half cited answering questions in class. If talking in class is an issue for you, these strategies might help:

- Set realistic goals for yourself; for example, asking one question per class period. Gradually build up to more demanding goals; for instance, not only asking pertinent questions, but also volunteering your opinions.
- Think ahead about questions you might be asked. Then jot down a few notes to help you remember possible talking points. You don't need to read your notes verbatim, but you can glance at them for help if you get stuck.
- Give yourself a pat on the back when you reach one of your goals. Remind yourself that talking in class will get easier with practice.

Giving a Presentation

Numerous studies have found that public speaking is the most commonly feared social situation. As a student, you'll probably be required to give some speeches or presentations for your classes, and eventually you might need to do the same for work. By overcoming the fear of public speaking, you may improve not only your grades now, but also your chances for career advancement later. If giving a speech or presentation brings out your anxiety, these strategies might help:

- Become comfortable with your topic. When given the option, pick a topic that genuinely interests you. Then prepare thoroughly. If you have a firm grasp of the material, that's one less thing you'll have to worry about.

- Try not to panic at the first sign of nerves. It's normal to feel a little nervous, especially during the first minute or so of your talk. Take a few deep breaths to relax your body and calm your mind. As you get some successful experiences under your belt, you'll start to believe in your ability to calm down.

- Join an organization such as Toastmasters International, which lets you hone your public speaking skills in front of a supportive audience.

- Seek out other opportunities to practice being at the center of attention. Volunteer to lead a club meeting or prayer group. Or if there's an issue you care deeply about, bring it up at your town's next city council or school board meeting.

Taking a Test

Test anxiety can have different causes, but sometimes it arises from performance anxiety—in other words, worry or fear about how you'll do on a specific task that's performed in front of others. Anxiety over tests also may be related to concerns about being judged by the teacher. This type of anxiety can take a serious toll on your grades even if you know the material well. When your mind is chock full of stressful thoughts and self doubts, it's hard to make room for thinking clearly and remembering what you know. If you're bothered by test anxiety, these strategies might help:

- Build up your confidence by preparing well for the test. Spread out your studying over several nights so you don't wind up frantically cramming the night before. In addition to studying on your own, consider joining a study group, which not only helps you prepare, but also gives you a chance to socialize.

- Help your brain function at its best. Get a good night's sleep the night before the test, and eat a healthy breakfast that morning. Just don't overdo the coffee, since a case of caffeine jitters definitely won't help your nerves.

- Be alert for automatic thoughts that undermine your self-confidence; for example, "I'm going to fail." Ask yourself whether these thoughts are accurate, and if not, replace them with more accurate thinking; for example, "I studied the chapter, and now I just need to do what I can. It's okay if I'm not perfect."

- Stop for a few moments and orient yourself in your surroundings when you start losing your train of thought during the test. One strategy is to notice the color of various items in the room. Take the time to say complete sentences to yourself, such as: The desk is brown. The walls are tan. The teacher's dress is orange and yellow. This strategy slows down your thinking and forces you to focus on something other than your anxiety. I've found it to be a great help.

Interacting With Other Students

Academics are only part of the whole school experience. For most students, socializing with classmates is at least as important, if not more so. But for those with social anxiety disorder, small talk is a tall order, made all the more excruciating by the ease with which other students seem to navigate the social maze. Truth be told, most of your fellow students probably feel out of place and self-conscious at times, too, and some may even have symptoms of social anxiety disorder. When you're wrapped up in your own misery, though, it's hard to see that you're not the only one. If you have trouble interacting with other students, these strategies might help:

...most of your fellow students probably feel out of place and self-conscious at times, too...

- Look for simple ways to get the ball rolling. Wave, smile, or just say "hi." As you grow more comfortable, try asking a question ("Are you going to the game tonight?") or making an observation ("That test was a killer").
- Practice making the appropriate amount of eye contact for the situation. In one-on-one conversation, that typically means alternating between short periods of looking the person straight in the eye and simply looking in the person's general direction. At first, this pattern of eye contact may feel a bit awkward if you're not used to it, but it will come more naturally with time. In my case, as I built up more confidence in other areas of my life, eye contact just seemed to fall into place.
- Don't expect everything you say to be witty or profound. Listen to other people's small talk, and you'll realize that it's often quite bland or even silly. Tell yourself, "I don't have to think of something important (or intelligent or fascinating) to say. As long as I say something, I'm making a connection."

Communicating With Your Teachers

If social anxiety disorder begins seriously interfering with your ability to get along at school, you might want to talk to your teacher or school counselor about the situation. While you may feel as if you're the only one with this problem, that's far from the case. Given how common social anxiety disorder is, many experienced teachers and counselors have run into other students with the disorder before. Some may be able to offer helpful suggestions and sensitive support.

However, because students with social anxiety disorder tend to be quiet and often go to great lengths not to draw attention to themselves, teachers may not be as aware of the problem as you would think. In addition, many teachers—like many people in society at large—confuse social anxiety disorder with ordinary shyness, so they might dismiss the problem too lightly or make suggestions that simply aren't workable for a student whose symptoms are severe.

Be ready to educate your educators, if necessary. While some teachers recognize social anxiety when they see it, they may not be familiar with the term social anxiety disorder or know exactly what it means. Others may be relatively oblivious to what you're going through or unaware of how deeply you're affected. If you're in treatment, your doctor or therapist might be able to provide some materials you can share. Also check out the Resources section at the end of this book. Many of the Web sites listed there provide articles you can print out and share with your teachers. Of course, you also can share this book. Most teachers are avid learners by nature, so there's a good chance you'll get a positive response to a few tactfully offered resources.

If your social anxiety at school is severe, you might need a helping hand to get your symptoms under control at first. If you're making changes in your behavior and still not seeing as much improvement as you had expected, consider asking for your teachers' help. That might mean making some temporary adjustments in what you're expected to do. The key is being very clear that you aren't seeking an unfair advantage. You also aren't looking for a way to keep avoiding the situations you fear indefinitely. All you're asking for are changes that let you start with easier challenges and gradually work up to harder ones—the fastest route to success in the long run. The exact changes you'll need depend on your situation, but the table below has examples of the kinds of adjustments that some students have found helpful.

When You Need a Helping Hand at School

Sometimes little changes can make a big difference in your ability to get along at school. These are examples of short-term changes that some students have found helpful while in the early stages of treatment. As treatment progresses, the need for these kinds of adjustments should gradually diminish and eventually disappear.

If you're extremely anxious about...	Then you might ask your teacher if he or she would consider...
Answering questions in class	• Using a signal that lets you know when your turn is coming so you can mentally prepare • Beginning with yes-no questions and gradually moving on to questions that call for longer responses
Making presentations	• Allowing you to make your presentation in front of just the teacher instead of the whole class • Letting you read from notes during your presentation
Taking tests	• Letting you take the test in private • Allowing you to substitute a portfolio

Your Educational Rights

Usually, a tactful request is enough to arrange for any simple, short-term changes you're likely to need at school. But if your situation is unusually complicated or you run into strong resistance, there are two federal laws you should know about: the Individuals with Disabilities Education Improvement Act of 2004 (IDEA) and Section 504 of the Rehabilitation Act of 1973. The information below applies to high school or younger students. For information about your rights as a college student, see the Frequently Asked Questions section at the end of this book.

- IDEA—To qualify for services under IDEA, you must show that you have a disability that impacts your ability to benefit from general educational services. This requires going through an evaluation and being given a label—in the case of social anxiety disorder, it means being labeled as having an "emotional disturbance" or "other health impairment." The process is lengthy and involved, so it's only appropriate if you have extensive, long-lasting needs. If you qualify, you'll receive an individualized education program (IEP)—a written educational plan that spells out how your individual needs will be met. For more details, visit the Web sites of the U.S. Department of Education (www.idea.ed.gov) or the Parent Advocacy Coalition for Educational Rights (www.pacer.org).
- Section 504—To qualify for services under Section 504, you must have a physical or mental impairment that substantially limits one or more major life activities. The 504 process is faster and more flexible than the one required under IDEA. In addition, there is sometimes less stigma attached to having a 504 plan than an IEP. IDEA is a better choice for students with extensive special needs. But Section 504 is often a good option when you have social anxiety disorder, which usually doesn't require a lot of costly, specialized services at school.

Another Ride on the Career Roller Coaster

With a master's degree in hand, my days as a student had reached an end, and it was time to move on to the next stage of my life. I decided to return to Washington, where I could resume face-to-face therapy sessions with Dr. Q. Besides giving me access to the Ross Center, the move also opened up vastly more work and social opportunities for me, since my hometown is very small, with a population of just 300 people. In addition, Dr. Q. thought the move would be a good idea because it would get me out of the stressful environment at my parent's house. And it would push me to become self-sufficient, rather than continuing to rely on my parents for everything from a roof over my head to transportation and spending money.

I searched online for apartment listings and job openings in the Washington area. After flying to an interview (which involved getting on a plane for the first time in five years, thanks to the help of Dr. Q.), I landed a job as a sixth-grade literacy teacher. I was thrilled. I knew that teaching would have its share of anxiety-provoking moments, but I also knew that I could rely on Dr. Q. for support. I moved to Washington in August of 2005, and right from the start, this move felt different from the others that had preceded it. For the first time in my life, it didn't feel as if I was running away to start over. It felt as if I was moving forward with confident strides.

I began the teaching job with energy and enthusiasm, as was my usual pattern in a new environment before I knew anybody or they knew me. This time, though, I was bent on continuing my progress, so I went out of my way to connect with co-workers, students, and parents. I made a point of wandering into other teachers' classrooms to compliment their curriculum, ask questions, and inquire about their classroom decorations. At open house, I initiated conversations with parents, volunteering information about the school before they even had a chance to ask.

After about three weeks, however, huge doubts began to surface. Despite having very little evidence to support this opinion,

I became convinced that no one was satisfied with my work, and I was sure that the entire faculty believed me to be incompetent. The simplest tasks, such as stepping into the teachers' room or monitoring student behavior in the lunchroom, suddenly felt like major ordeals.

To staff, students, and parents, I tried to keep up the illusion that I was on top of everything. By working nonstop at school and home, I believed that I could keep others from accusing me of not being good at my job—or at least, of not trying. I outdid myself at every turn, working day and night. Even on weekends, I was at the computer for hours making lesson plans, recording grades, and generally trying to live up to my own ridiculously high standards for being an outstanding teacher. But no matter how hard I tried, I couldn't shake the fear of being fired.

...I tried to keep up the illusion that I was on top of everything.

Social anxiety is often described as a "fear of negative evaluation," but something gets lost in that translation. While it's an accurate description, it doesn't fully convey the emotional impact of living every moment in dread. Everything I did—from talking to another teacher about a scheduled fire drill to being observed in my classroom by the principal—carried with it the same assumption that I was about to say or do something wrong.

I was guilty of not being in the present moment, of always thinking ahead to the point when a lesson would veer off track and my supervisor would walk in to see it. If I reprimanded a student, I anticipated the moment when I would receive a message that an angry parent had called the principal to complain. If two teachers passed in the hallway, I feared they might be talking about what a poor teacher I was.

Because I had Dr. Q.'s support, I managed not to sink immediately into the state I had reached when teaching three years before. And when the day finally came that I was feeling ready to walk out of the school and never go back, I summoned up the courage to call Dr. Q.'s office and ask for an emergency appointment.

Dr. Q. helped me schedule a visit that day with a physician who accepted walk-in patients. I told the doctor why I was there and that I was already taking bupropion (Wellbutrin), an antidepressant that's chemically unrelated to SSRIs and SNRIs. (Wellbutrin has not been shown to be effective against social anxiety disorder, but it can help with depression.) The doctor wrote me a prescription for a three-month supply of the anti-anxiety drug buspirone (BuSpar). This new medicine took some of the edge off the anxiety, but there wasn't a dramatic change. Meanwhile, I tried to follow Dr. Q.'s advice to distract myself evenings and weekends with non-school-related activities. But my attempts at distraction were half-hearted, and I continued to struggle.

Between October and November, I tried to quit my job no less than three times. Each time, I was shocked when told by my supervisors that I was doing a fine job and should stay on. Eventually, though, the stress became too much. In November of 2005, I approached the principal with a letter of resignation, and for the first time, I explained to someone for whom I worked that I had social anxiety disorder. I told her that I would stay until the end of December, but then I would be leaving.

On my last day, I received a surprise card signed by over two dozen of my coworkers. I stood alone amid the boxes in my classroom and choked back tears as I read the messages inside:

Emily, it was great to work with you. Your dedication and creativity with your class pushed me to do the same.—Ms. M.

Emily, good luck with everything you do in the future. You brought a real positive light to the English Department and will truly be missed.   —Ms. C.

Emily, I wish you the best in your future endeavors! We will miss you around here! You'll always be welcome in the C— community.   —Ms. F., Principal

Steady Progress at Last

I found myself with a choice to make. I could once again try to erase a painful experience from my memory, leave Washington in defeat, and move back to my parents' home in New York. Or I could confront the anxious feelings that had caused me to leave yet another job. This time around, I chose the second option. I had come too far to give up, and I was determined to continue the work that I was doing with Dr. Q. in order to deal with my irrational feelings of incompetence in the workplace.

By March of 2006, I had eased my way back into employment, working as a nanny first three days a week, then four. I soon developed a comfortable relationship with my employer, something I had never been able to do in the past. Several months later, I accepted a second job, leading tours for children at the National Zoo on weekends. Within a month of taking the zoo job, I was promoted to supervisor. For the first time in my life, I felt confident about the work I was doing, and I was finally able to strike a balance between work and leisure activities.

For the first time in my life, I felt confident about the work I was doing...

After years of ups and downs, my career is now on a steady course. Returning to the classroom is an option that I keep open. As time goes on and I build my confidence, I may re-explore teaching or even look into other careers in the field of English. I may never feel 100 percent ready, but by regularly reexamining my thinking and challenging myself when necessary, I know the time will come when I'll possess the self-assurance to face the atmosphere of a busy workplace.

For now, my social anxiety hasn't completely disappeared, but I'm handling it better by applying the same kinds of strategies that worked in other settings. When I catch myself having negative thoughts, I go back to my mantra: Where's the evidence? And when I find that the negative thoughts are exaggerated or unjustified, as they often are, I make a conscious effort to replace them with more realistic thinking.

Dealing With Social Anxiety at Work

Many of the demands of the workplace are similar to those at school. As a result, many of the same coping strategies can be applied. For instance, I discovered that I could use some of the same tactics that helped me speak up more during my last college course to cope with my anxiety during later job interviews.

One question that sometimes comes up is whether to tell your boss about your social anxiety disorder. This is a very personal decision that only you can make. Just keep in mind that some bosses are more enlightened about mental illness than others, so use your judgment about how much information to share and when. If you do choose to discuss your disorder, keep the focus positive. Talk about how reasonable adjustments can help you be more successful at your job, not how anxiety might cause you to fail.

Personally, I have made the decision not to tell most of my employers about my condition. As I see it, feeling the effects of the disorder is unavoidable at work, but I am the one who's responsible for managing my own symptoms. The more I ask others to make allowances for me, the less I am dealing with the harsh feelings I need to learn to face.

I *will* tell a prospective employer, however, if gaps in my resume are noted during a job interview. At that point, I will be honest about my history with social anxiety disorder and share my true feelings about my competency to fill the job. I let the interviewer know that, although some social interactions may be difficult for me on a personal level, I am capable of handling them professionally.

Without treatment, social anxiety disorder can make it very difficult to function at work, as my early job history shows. It can keep you from getting the job you deserve, undermine your work performance, and block your path to promotion. As the pressure mounts, just showing up at work each day can start to seem like an insurmountable hurdle. But I'm here to tell you that it's a hurdle you can get over with hard work, determination, and appropriate treatment. There was a time when I almost despaired of having a rewarding career, but now I know differently. Social anxiety may be a challenge in the workplace, but that doesn't mean it has to stand in the way of your dreams.

Sticking With the Program

Facing your fears is critical, but maintaining your progress is even more important for long-term well-being. Social anxiety disorder sometimes lessens or even disappears in adulthood. For many people, though, it's a lifelong condition. The symptoms often come and go, getting worse during times of stress, but they may never go away completely.

That doesn't mean you're doomed to misery and solitude if you have the disorder, however. Treatment can help you manage your symptoms and take back control of your life. If your symptoms do reemerge, you'll know what is happening, how to cope effectively on your own, and where to find professional help when you need it.

If you have a setback now and then, don't let it throw you.

If you have a setback now and then, don't let it throw you. Even when you've lost considerable ground, you may be able to regain it quickly by drawing upon the skills you previously learned. Try to keep the situation in perspective. A setback might be a step backward, but it doesn't eradicate all the forward steps you've already taken.

Remember that practice makes progress. Commit to taking on fresh challenges and learning new social skills. If you keep putting yourself into situations that cause anxiety and staying there until the anxiety subsides, you'll find that your comfort zone naturally expands over time.

What I Learned From Group Therapy

As part of my personal commitment to ongoing improvement, I agreed to Dr. Q.'s suggestion that I attend a few group therapy sessions for socially anxious adults. I'll admit to feeling reluctant at first, but that feeling soon changed to pleasant surprise as I discovered that there were other people, normal people, with worries similar to mine.

One young woman I met there had recently dropped out of college because the social demands of her psychology major were too great. Another woman, a lawyer, found interacting with coworkers to be a constant struggle. A third woman, a dancer with the talent to work professionally, was considering giving up her dream because of extreme performance anxiety.

Joining a Support Group

Support groups are another great place to practice your social skills. They're different from group therapy in that the members aren't working toward formal treatment goals, and the meetings aren't necessarily led by a mental health professional. Instead, support groups are more like a club where all the members share a common problem. Meetings are a place to offer support, voice concerns, and talk about practical strategies for dealing with real-life social situations. They're also a source of inspiration, since there's nothing more encouraging than getting to know other people who have fought the same battles as you and won. Plus, such groups are a great place to find new friends. The Anxiety Disorders Association of America has a list of anxiety-related support groups on its Web site (www.adaa.org/GettingHelp/SupportGroups.asp).

Men were represented, too. In fact, more than half of the group members were men whose social anxiety was affecting their advancement in careers as artists, architects, and engineers.

By taking part in activities such as these, I've become better at expressing my true, unrehearsed thoughts and feelings on the spot. I've discovered that people often don't find my ideas that strange after all.

I recently confessed to Dr. Q. that I was afraid to write e-mails to her when I was feeling especially stressed or down, because I was worried about how my thoughts might come across. Her response was reassuring: "If they are, as you say, 'weird,' 'odd,' or 'crazy,' then by sharing what you're thinking, we at least have something to work with. But I haven't heard you say anything crazy yet."

Chapter Eight

My Life Today, Your Life Tomorrow

As a child, Emily was incomparable, unusual, even precocious.
At age four she was writing little poems and stories, enjoying
music, art, and a myriad of creative pastimes. The breadth of
her imagination along with her joie de vivre *was a charming*
combination. Then in her teens, Emily became increasingly self-
conscious. Immediate post-college days marked the beginning of
her deep depression. I think of it as her dark period. During
this time she frequently slept by day and was up all night. Emo-
tional reactions were almost nonexistent. Emily withdrew socially;
personal interactions became rare. Anxiety plagued her to the
point of refusing to talk on the phone, which, of course, was a
detriment to work situations. Her eating habits became bizarre,
eating all oatmeal one week, and toast and coffee the next. Re-
markably, Emily has abandoned her dark despair and reemerged
into the radiance of self-delight and that of the world around
her. Of her own accord she found and put herself under the aegis
of an anxiety treatment center. Through psychotherapy and
medication Emily has become a "new" person, ironically by be-
coming her "old" self. Once again Emily has embraced the validity

of her emotions, her uniqueness and her interest in the lives of others.

—Mom

When given the opportunity to share my experiences in a book about social anxiety disorder, I questioned how reading my story could possibly benefit anyone. I feared that the book would only set me further apart and make my struggle seem different from everybody else's. I also worried about reader skepticism. If I had been given a similar book years ago, I might have handed it right back, thinking that no one who truly had social anxiety disorder would write a book putting her most personal thoughts, feelings, and experiences on display. Writing a book requires one to confer, edit, and get regular feedback. And what person with social anxiety would assume that others were interested in reading his or her story anyway?

Yet that's exactly what I've done in these pages. I would be less than truthful if I said it was easy. I didn't want to come across as someone who used her past as a crutch or wanted credit for not giving up when she felt she had come to the end of her rope. I plainly wanted readers to know that there's a lot to social anxiety disorder that doesn't get printed in every article, maybe because it isn't always pretty or easy to explain. I wanted readers to know that it is possible to overcome the disorder, but it takes time and true effort.

I wanted readers to know that it is possible to overcome the disorder...

At one point, I avoided the sight of my computer, afraid that I was writing a lie. How much progress had I truly made? I was going through a tough time, and in my therapy sessions with Dr. Q., I was doing little more than smiling and gazing downward. Eventually, I hit a low that I hadn't felt in a long time. Fearing that I had completely relapsed, I broke down and told Dr. Q. exactly how I was feeling. Suddenly, the good feelings of accomplishment from the first days of therapy came rushing back. I had just done something very difficult yet again by opening myself up, crying in Dr. Q.'s office, and telling her what I was truly feeling.

This may sound like a simple act, but it required trusting that Dr. Q. wouldn't think my most personal thoughts were orchestrated ploys for pity. I dug deep and found the trust, and the results were amazing. Just by letting down my defenses and being honest, my energy returned, and my self-esteem was bolstered. I realized then that I *had* overcome a great deal. My faith in recovery—and in this book—was restored.

Throughout the book, my aim has been to give social anxiety disorder a real face and to share the plain facts of how it has affected me. Rather than a straight uphill course, my road to recovery has been filled with twists and turns, along with a few gigantic potholes. Yet in spite of finding no miraculous cures and enduring several setbacks, I *did* get better—and you can, too, with hard work and proper treatment.

Perfectly Fine Imperfect Me

When I was a teenager, I longed for my life to be as picture-perfect as the back-to-school ads in magazines. In my fantasies, I always sported a sly smile and a fantastic hairstyle, and I was posed with casual indifference against a wall of lockers, surrounded by a group of playful, good-looking admirers.

As you've seen by now, however, my reality was a stark contrast to the fantasized image. When I couldn't achieve that particular picture of perfection, I began trying to squeeze myself into a series of other idealized images: the hermit philosopher, the beloved teacher, the undiscovered writer. Nothing fit just right—nor would it until I finally realized that perfection wasn't "out there." I had to learn that satisfaction with myself came from within. Ultimately, I had to come to terms with the idea that it's perfectly fine to be imperfect, to ask for help, and not to know all the answers.

Today I continue pushing myself to take on new challenges, even though that inevitably means risking mistakes. When I'm cringing at the thought of my potential humiliation, I remember that putting myself on the line is the only way I can keep making progress. I try to stay "in the moment" and express what I'm feeling when I'm feeling it, without worrying about how I might embarrass myself later on. And if I do, in fact, make an embarrassing mistake, I remind myself to just keep going.

By now, I've embarrassed myself in front of Dr. Q. so many times that I've lost count. (Once, when she told me to ask her any question I wanted, I actually asked what her living room looked like!) But I've also reaped the rewards of taking risks. In fact, one reason I had the opportunity to write this book is because I risked showing Dr. Q. a paper on social anxiety that I had written as a junior in college.

Dispelling Myths and Fighting Stigma

One of the challenges I'm taking on by writing this book is dispelling the many myths that surround social anxiety disorder. There's a tendency to think of social anxiety as an imaginary ailment or character flaw rather than a real illness. As a result, people who would never criticize someone for having asthma or diabetes can sometimes be surprisingly insensitive where social anxiety disorder is concerned. When I encounter this type of attitude, I try to keep in mind that it's not a reflection on me. It's a reflection of the other person's lack of awareness. At times like these, it helps me to remember that *I am not responsible for other people's actions or behavior.*

Many people never stop to think that the brain is just another organ of the body, and like other organs, it's vulnerable to disease. Often they may be more understanding once you point out that the psychological symptoms of social anxiety disorder are based in physiological changes in the brain.

...the brain is just another organ of the body, and like other organs, it's vulnerable to disease.

Being assertive doesn't come naturally to many people with social anxiety disorder, but it's a skill worth cultivating. When you hear people cracking cruel jokes or making unkind remarks about mental illness, it will do you both good if you tactfully let the other person know that you find this unacceptable. It's not a matter of political correctness. It's a matter of basic respect. Once again, most people aren't intentionally being hurtful. They just haven't given the issue much thought, and by bringing it to their attention, you're doing them a favor.

Once you start speaking out, you may be surprised by how many people come up to thank you or share their own stories. According to the National Institute of Mental Health, over 57 million U.S. adults suffer from a mental illness in any given year. In addition, it's estimated that one out of every ten children and teenagers has a mental disorder severe enough to cause impairment. Now add all the parents, siblings, teachers, classmates, friends, neighbors, and coworkers of those with mental illness, and it's easy to see that almost everyone is touched by mental illness either directly or indirectly. You have a lot of people in your corner.

Taking a Chance on Friendship

While social anxiety disorder *is* an illness, simply blaming the disease won't improve your condition. Sometimes in life, you're dealt a bad hand, but the goal is to win the game. By learning about social anxiety, adopting healthy diet and exercise habits, being responsible about taking your medication, and participating actively in therapy, your life with social anxiety disorder can be more than bearable. It can be wonderful.

Today I have a close friend because I took a chance not once, but several times. I accompanied her to coffee shops and bookstores even after I had convinced myself that she was only going with me to be polite. (I was wrong; she did like me.) I've continued going out and kept telephoning in spite of moments when I felt as though I'd said the wrong thing, been exceptionally boring, or made an utter fool of myself. I pushed myself to open up and occasionally talk about me, instead of relying on my tendency to put the other person in the spotlight, asking question after question. Over time, it got easier, and making friends became less work and more fun.

As for romantic relationships, more than ever before I see marriage and a family as a possibility in my future. For years, I had lost all interest in dating. On the rare occasions when I went out, I tended to be outgoing at first, then made up excuses when asked to go out again. Once on a date, I did everything that I thought the other person wanted me to do. If he wanted to hold hands, we held hands. If he initiated a kiss, we kissed. If he wanted to drive me home, he drove me home. I never gave voice to my wants, safety concerns, or reservations about the relationship.

When I go on dates today (and yes, I've made the happy discovery that I am interested in dating again), I'm not nervously out to please. My purpose is to meet someone and enjoy myself in the process. If we don't hit it off, I don't automatically assume it's because I am too boring or ugly, or that I must have broken some first-date code of conduct. Never do I put my safety in jeopardy, no matter how awkward it feels to say no or refuse a ride. If I don't feel comfortable doing so much as shaking hands, that's my right to decide. The nice part about dating in my late twenties, as opposed to my teens, is that appearances and popularity aren't as important as they were in high school. At 27, it's easier to date for the sake of genuine companionship, not for the pressure of being seen with the "right" person.

Building a Better Future

When it comes to work, I still haven't found a job that will offer me financial security and health benefits, but I'm thrilled that I'm finally able to pay my own way. At times, it astonishes me to think of how far I've come in just the last year. It was only months ago when I believed that waking up in the morning without an intense fear of facing my supervisors and co-workers was an unachievable dream. Yet here I am! I love what I do, and I take pride in doing it well.

Recently, I did the unthinkable: I joined a gym. A regular exercise routine coupled with a balanced diet has done wonders for my mood. At first, it was intimidating to learn how to use the equipment, and there were times when I felt out of place among the athletic women in the locker room. But although my level of anxiety often starts out as an 8 or 9, it goes down to a 7 as soon as I'm dressed, and once I get going on my workout, it's down to a 5 or 6.

All the same, it was a shock to step into the locker room one morning and find Dr. Q. there getting ready for her workout.

"What secrets could we possibly have from one another now?" she joked.

Very few, I thought.

I still have appointments with Dr. Q. every few weeks, and she continues to give me encouragement as well as assignments. The CBT techniques I've learned from Dr. Q. have been invaluable. However, I believe that the trusting relationship I've formed with her has been just as important to my recovery. During the time I have been in treatment with Dr. Q., I've taken strength from her support and reassurance from knowing she'll be there for me in a crisis. My sessions with her have given me a safe place to practice my relationship and personal-sharing skills. And thanks to the bond I've forged with Dr. Q., I have new faith in my ability to have an open, honest relationship with other people.

At times, I get discouraged when I backslide a little or find that my progress is going more slowly than I would like. Then I remind myself that Rome wasn't built in a day, and neither was my personality. It took me 27 years to get to this point, and it's okay if it takes me a few more days, weeks, or even months to reach the next milestone.

Social anxiety disorder is just one of the many characteristics that make me the unique person I am. My goal is not so much to overcome social anxiety as to lead the happiest, healthiest, most rewarding life I can. Fortunately, I've found that the kinds of lifestyle changes that are good for reducing my social anxiety are also good for improving my overall well-being—mentally, physically, and socially.

> Social anxiety disorder is just one of the many characteristics that make me the unique person I am.

Today I'm out of my apartment by quarter of six in the morning to make time for breakfast at the same café where I purchased the fateful blueberry yogurt over a year and a half ago. Like many people, I go to work, come home, pay bills, and tend to my pets. Some nights, I'll go to the gym. Other nights, I'll go shopping. I've joined a book club, and on Fridays, I go to dinner with a friend of mine. We are in the planning stages of sharing an apartment, and we are even exploring the possibility of starting a business together. I don't know what the future will hold, but I'm optimistic. Social anxiety is, and perhaps always will be, a factor in many of my decisions, but it doesn't dictate my life. I no longer define myself solely in terms of social anxiety disorder.

Writing Your Own Happy Ending

My advice to you is to do what you can today. If you haven't yet asked for help, let this be the day you do. Talk to someone now about how you're feeling. Don't wait for the perfect setting or moment. Chances are, it won't play out like the scene in your head anyway. You probably won't be wearing the right clothes or standing at the right spot in the room. You may stammer your way through describing your feelings instead of giving the beautiful speech you had planned. And when you're finished, you might not get the word-for-word response you're longing to hear.

Don't walk away. Do your best to stand your ground and talk about your feelings. If it makes you more comfortable, jot down some notes ahead of time so you don't lose sight of the most important points you want to make. It also may help to do some advance research about social anxiety disorder. Having solid information at hand may help get the conversation rolling.

If the first person you approach doesn't understand or doesn't seem to take your situation seriously, try someone else.

Be persistent until you get the help you need. Your parents are probably at the top of the list of people to confide in, but other good sources of advice and assistance include your family doctor, teacher, school counselor, school nurse, or religious advisor.

If I had been given a choice of either getting help for social anxiety sooner or living through it so I could write a book about my experiences, I would definitely have taken the first option. Although I'm not ashamed of my history, I missed out on a lot, and I put unnecessary hurdles in my path.

The bravest choice you can make is to ask for help.

The fewer obstacles you have in front of you, the sooner you'll be able to do all the things you want to do. The bravest choice you can make is to ask for help. But don't feel like you have to face this challenge alone. Caring, knowledgeable people are ready and willing to provide the support you need.

Frequently Asked Questions

Coping With Social Anxiety

What's the difference between social phobia and social anxiety disorder?

You're likely to run across both terms when looking for information about social anxiety. Don't let that throw you. The terms *social phobia* and *social anxiety disorder* mean the same thing and are used interchangeably.

I've been trying to confront my fears, but I'm still feeling very anxious in some situations. What am I doing wrong?

Instead of thinking about what you're doing wrong, why not focus on what you're doing right? You've taken those first steps toward facing your fears, and that requires a lot of courage. The fact that you're not giving up even when it's difficult shows that you have the necessary determination to succeed. That being said, some problems are undeniably harder to solve than others. It may take a little extra creativity and effort to overcome your most persistent anxieties.

In some cases, you might not be putting yourself into the anxiety-provoking situation often enough. Practice, practice, practice is the key to becoming more comfortable in social situations. But some situations don't arise very often, so you might need to go out of your way to find enough opportunities to practice facing them. For example, let's say you have an annual piano recital coming up, and you know from past experience that performance anxiety is a problem for you. There are a couple of rehearsals right before the recital, but otherwise you rarely play in front of anyone other than your piano teacher. To get more practice performing for an audience, you might make a point of playing at family and neighborhood gatherings. You also might volunteer as a pianist for your school chorus or drama club. Or you could share your musical talent at church, or offer to entertain at a local daycare center or nursing home. Any place with a piano is a potential practice stage for you.

In other cases, you might be getting plenty of exposure to the anxiety-provoking situation, but then doing things that undermine your efforts. For instance, you may be going to social events, but then always talking to the same people once you get there. Or you might be doing a perfectly fine job of confronting your fears, but then deflating your self-confidence with negative thoughts afterward.

If you continue to feel anxious despite your best efforts, that's just a signal to call in the reinforcements. A mental health professional can help you get over these kinds of difficult hurdles. If you're already in treatment, don't hesitate to talk with your doctor or therapist about any problems you're encountering. And if you haven't reached out for professional help yet, now might be the time.

I'd like to ask one of my classmates on a date, but anxiety keeps getting in the way. How can I overcome my anxiety?

Try to keep the situation in perspective. You aren't looking for someone to marry; you're just looking for a friend to share a pizza with or a date for the school dance. If you ask out your classmate, there's probably a decent chance he or she will accept. But even if the answer is no, it's not the end of the world, and it's also not a sign that there's something terribly wrong with you. Maybe the other person doesn't like pizza or dancing, or maybe he or she is already dating someone else. This is really a no-lose proposition for you, though, because whatever the outcome, you've had a chance to practice your social skills. The next time you ask someone out, it will come easier. Eventually, you'll start to feel and sound more confident, and most people find confidence very attractive.

Some teenagers feel as if they must perfect themselves before they try dating. For example, you might think you need to clear up your acne first, lose ten pounds, or buy better clothes. While it makes sense to take care of your appearance, a quick glance around shows that all kinds of people—including people with pimples, different sizes and shapes of bodies, and non-designer clothes—can and do go on dates. If you have a long-term goal to improve your appearance, that's fine, but it doesn't mean you have to put off your social life in the meantime.

I get very anxious about talking on the phone. How can I manage this fear?

As you know by now, getting over my own fear of using the phone was a big issue for me. Just as with face-to-face conversations, the key is facing your fear over and over until your anxiety fades. At first, you might practice making phone calls that have a specific, not-too-threatening purpose. For example, you might call certain stores to ask what hours they're open or phone a classmate to ask about when the homework assignment is due. If you think it would help, you can even write out a script to guide you through those first few calls. Over time, you can gradually work up to making more challenging calls on the spur of the moment.

It's so embarrassing when I blush in front of everyone. How can I control my blushing?

In truth, it's more the fear of blushing than the redness itself that is a problem. As your overall anxiety and self-consciousness decrease, the fear—and consequently, the blushing—should lessen. In the meantime, you can work on challenging your negative thoughts. Keep in mind that you are probably far more aware of your blushing than anyone else is. Then remind yourself that those who do notice have undoubtedly blushed, too, so they may empathize more than you think. In fact, occasional blushing is a normal part of life, or as Charles Darwin put it, "the most human of all expressions." It can even be attractive, which is why girls use makeup to fake pink cheeks.

Getting Effective Treatment

There are so many kinds of mental health professionals who provide psychotherapy. What's the difference between one type of therapist and another?

This is a common source of confusion. Psychotherapy can be provided by professionals from several fields, including psychiatry, psychology, social work, psychiatric nursing, and counseling. Each field has its own licensure requirements, which vary somewhat from state to state. In addition, the various disciplines differ in their basic orientation and training requirements. Below is a quick rundown of some key differences:

- *Psychiatrists* (M.D.) are medical doctors. After graduating from medical school, they spend the first year of residency training on taking care of patients with a range of medical conditions, then at least three years of residency after that specializing in mental illnesses. Many psychiatrists are board certified by the American Board of Psychiatry and Neurology, an important indicator of quality. In addition, some psychiatrists undertake further training in child and adolescent psychiatry. While some psychiatrists provide therapy, others focus mainly on prescribing and monitoring drug therapy, often working closely with therapists from other fields.
- *Psychologists* (Ph.D., Psy.D., Ed.D.) receive training that includes earning a doctoral degree as well as completing a supervised clinical internship and at least one year of post-doctoral supervised experience. Some psychologists are board certified specifically in cognitive and behavioral psychology by the American Board of Professional Psychology.
- *Clinical social workers* (M.S.W., D.S.W., Ph.D.) hold a master's degree or above. To be certified by the Academy of Certified Social Workers, they also must have two years of post-degree experience. More than other therapists, clinical social workers are trained in patient advocacy. When appropriate, some provide assistance in getting help from government agencies.

- *Psychiatric nurses* (A.P.R.N.) are advanced practice registered nurses with a master's degree in psychiatric-mental health nursing. Some receive specialized training in child-adolescent mental health nursing. Certification is provided by the American Nurses Credentialing Center.
- *Professional counselors* (M.A., M.S., M.Ed., Ph.D., Ed.D.) hold a master's degree or above. In addition, licensed mental health counselors must have two years of post-degree experience. Some counselors are credentialed as certified clinical mental health counselors by the National Board for Certified Counselors. Many combine traditional psychotherapy with a practical problem-solving approach.

What kinds of treatment providers can prescribe medication?

Any medical doctor can prescribe medication for treating anxiety. However, psychiatrists are the physicians with the most training and experience when it comes to treating mental disorders with medication and monitoring the effects. Depending on where you live, certain other mental health professionals may be able to prescribe medication for mental disorders as well. Advanced practice psychiatric nurses can prescribe medication in many states. In addition, New Mexico and Louisiana allow licensed psychologists with appropriate training and certification to write prescriptions.

I don't like the idea of taking medicine. Is there an herbal supplement I can take instead?

Unfortunately, there isn't enough scientific evidence to know for sure whether popular supplements, such as kava and

St. John's wort, are effective for treating anxiety. In the case of kava, several small studies have suggested that it might help a little, but rigorous studies in larger groups of people are still needed. In the case of St. John's wort, there is some evidence that it might help mild depression, but no convincing evidence for anxiety. And contrary to what many people think, taking supplements isn't necessarily risk free. Any herb that's powerful enough to help your anxiety is also strong enough to potentially cause side effects. Plus, some herbal supplements may interact harmfully with certain prescription medications.

Kava has been linked to a risk of severe liver damage, especially in people who already have liver problems and those who are taking drugs that can affect the liver. St. John's wort can cause side effects such as increased sensitivity to sunlight, dry mouth, dizziness, upset stomach, fatigue, headaches, sexual problems, and even increased anxiety. These effects may be heightened when St. John's wort is combined with an antidepressant.

The bottom line: It doesn't make sense to use an herbal supplement with unproven benefits *in place of* a proven treatment. If you're interested in trying a supplement *along with* medication or psychotherapy, it's still smart to talk with your doctor first to make sure the treatments are compatible.

How can I work up the nerve to talk to a doctor or therapist about my symptoms for the first time?

The first visit to a new treatment provider can be a scary situation for someone with social anxiety disorder. It may help to bring a written list of your symptoms. Look back at the "Red Flags to Watch For" in Chapter 3, and list those that apply to you. Then add any other symptoms you may have noticed, keeping in mind that no two people experience social anxiety disorder in exactly the same way. You might find that your first visit goes more smoothly than expected. But if you do get rattled, you can read from your list, which takes some of the pressure off.

How do I tell my doctor or therapist about my symptoms if I'm too embarrassed to describe them?

This is a problem I have struggled with myself. I used to wonder a lot about what my therapist's other patients said and did, and I worried that my own words and actions might seem too odd or extreme by comparison. I often was tempted to recite the symptoms I thought I was supposed to have rather than describe the deeply personal and sometimes disturbing feelings I really was having.

These days, when I catch myself thinking that way, I remind myself that Dr. Q. isn't there to judge; she's there to listen and help. In order to help me effectively, she needs to have the straight facts. Chances are, she has already heard it all—or at least heard similar things—anyway. And contrary to my fears, Dr. Q. has never once seemed horrified or disgusted by anything I said.

Once you've confided something personal to your therapist, watch out for feelings of embarrassment that might make you want to avoid going back again. If such feelings do arise, remember that they're a reflection of your social anxiety, not a sign that you actually have anything to be embarrassed about. Second-guessing yourself is second nature when you have social anxiety. But as time goes on, you'll start to see that the more honest you are in therapy, the more benefit you gain.

Life Beyond High School

I'll be leaving for college soon. Will I be able to adjust to all the social demands there?

First of all, remember that you're not alone. In a recent survey by the American College Health Association, 14% of college students said they had experienced some form of anxiety within the last year. That's not surprising, because going to college is a big transition. While it's an exciting change, it's also potentially stressful, and stress can trigger symptoms of an anxiety disorder. Nevertheless, many students with social anxiety disorder meet the challenges of college successfully, and you can, too, by thinking ahead and lining up support in advance.

Think about how you can translate the coping strategies that have worked well in high school to a college setting. If you're currently in therapy or on medication, talk to your treatment provider about how you'll keep up your treatment while at college. If you're moving away to school and need to find a new doctor or therapist there, ask your current treatment provider to help you locate one, or contact the student counseling center or campus medical center for a referral.

Plan ahead for ways to connect with other students as well. On most campuses, you'll find student groups geared to a wide range of interests, from computers and art to politics and social causes. Push yourself to attend some meetings. In addition, many campuses host mental health support and advocacy groups. Two of the larger ones are Active Minds (www.activemindsoncampus.org) and NAMI on Campus (www.nami.org), but ask what's available at your school.

I'm a current college student who's struggling with
severe social anxiety. What are my educational
rights while I work on getting my symptoms
under control?

Some students with severe social anxiety disorder qualify as having a disability under the law. Section 504 of the Rehabilitation Act of 1973 applies to students in college as well as to younger students. Another law that applies to students at all levels is Title II of the Americans with Disabilities Act of 1990. Both of these laws prohibit discrimination on the basis of a disability, which is defined as an impairment that substantially limits one or more major life activities. However, there are some key changes in your educational rights once you graduate from high school.

Section 504 requires school districts to provide a "free appropriate public education" to each young person in their jurisdiction up through high school age. After high school, this requirement no longer applies. But colleges can't deny you admission simply because of a disability, assuming you otherwise meet their standards to get in. Colleges also must provide appropriate academic adjustments to ensure that they don't discriminate on the basis of a disability.

There are limits on the types of adjustments that colleges are required to make, however. Examples of possible adjustments include reducing your course load, substituting one course for another, or allowing extra time for taking tests. To make such arrangements, you'll need to notify the school that you have a disability and go through the school's procedure for requesting an academic adjustment, which can take some time. You'll probably need to provide documentation, such as a report from your treatment provider, to show that you have a disability that's affecting you at school. For more information, contact the U.S. Department of Education's Office for Civil Rights (800-421-3481, www.ed.gov/ocr).

Should I look into careers that don't require much social interaction?

My personal advice is to pursue the career you really want, at least as a long-term goal. The more you love your work, the more inspired you'll be to overcome social anxiety disorder. Realistically, however, you might need to make some short-term concessions while you address your symptoms. In addition, I think it's a good idea for anyone, social anxiety disorder or not, to stay flexible and open to unexpected opportunities. In my case, for example, I'm putting my education degree and love of children to good use. But rather than using them as a teacher the way I had expected, I'm currently using them as a nanny and a guide of children's zoo tours.

Will I eventually have a career, a family, and all the things I've dreamed of?

That's up to you, but there's no reason why social anxiety disorder has to hold you back. Yes, social anxiety makes life a bit more challenging, but by rising to the challenge, you'll develop pride and a sense of accomplishment. You'll also discover just how courageous and capable you really are, and the self-confidence you gain will serve you well, now and for the rest of your life.

Glossary

amygdala A small structure inside the brain that plays a key role in emotional memory and the fear response.

anorexia nervosa An eating disorder in which people have an intense fear of becoming fat, so they severely restrict what they eat, often to the point of near-starvation.

antidepressant A medication used to prevent or relieve depression. Antidepressants are also commonly used to treat anxiety disorders.

anxiety disorder Any of a group of mental disorders characterized by excessive fear or worry that is recurrent or long lasting. The symptoms of the disorder cause distress or interfere with day-to-day activities.

behavioral inhibition A pattern of timid, fearful behavior around strangers or new situations.

benzodiazepine An antianxiety medication that is thought to raise levels of gamma-amino-butyric acid in the brain.

bulimia nervosa An eating disorder in which people binge on large quantities of food, then purge by forced vomiting, laxative or diuretic abuse, or excessive exercise.

buspirone (BuSpar) The only medication intended specifically for treating anxiety that isn't a benzodiazepine. It increases serotonin activity in the brain.

cognitive-behavioral therapy (CBT) A form of psychotherapy that helps people recognize and change self-defeating thought patterns as well as identify and change maladaptive behaviors.

comorbid conditions Two or more disorders that coexist in the same individual.

depression A mental disorder that involves being in a low mood nearly all the time, or losing interest or enjoyment in almost everything.

Diagnostic and Statistical Manual of Mental Disorders, Fourth Edition, Text Revision (DSM-IV-TR)   The standard diagnostic manual used by mental health professionals.

dopamine   A neurotransmitter that enables movement and influences motivation and the perception of reality.

exposure therapy   A form of cognitive-behavioral therapy in which people systematically confront the situations that frighten them, working up from less threatening situations to more threatening ones.

gamma-amino-butyric acid (GABA)   A neurotransmitter that inhibits the activity of nerve cells and seems to help quell anxiety.

generalized anxiety disorder   An anxiety disorder characterized by constant worry over a number of different things.

generalized social anxiety disorder   Social anxiety that occurs in most social situations.

group therapy   Psychotherapy conducted in a small group that is led by a therapist and composed of other people with similar problems.

individualized education program (IEP)   A written educational plan for a student who qualifies for services under the Individuals with Disabilities Education Improvement Act of 2004.

Individuals with Disabilities Education Improvement Act of 2004 (IDEA)   A federal law that applies to students who have a disability that impacts their ability to benefit from general educational services.

introversion   A general tendency toward having a quiet, reserved nature.

Medicaid   A government program that provides health insurance to eligible low-income and disabled individuals.

medical necessity   A standard used by many insurance plans in determining whether to pay for a health care service. To satisfy this standard, the service must be deemed medically appropriate and necessary to meet a patient's health care needs.

monoamine oxidase inhibitor (MAOI)   An antidepressant that simultaneously raises serotonin, norepinephrine, and dopamine levels in the brain.

neurotransmitter   A chemical that acts as a messenger inside the brain.

obsessive-compulsive disorder   An anxiety disorder characterized by recurrent, uncontrollable, intrusive thoughts (obsessions), or actions that the person feels driven to perform in response to these thoughts (compulsions).

panic attack   A sudden, unexpected wave of intense fear and apprehension that's accompanied by physical symptoms, such as a racing or pounding heart, shortness of breath, sweating, trembling, chest pain, or choking sensations.

panic disorder   An anxiety disorder characterized by the repeated occurrence and fear of spontaneous panic attacks.

performance anxiety   Stress and worry or fear about how you will perform on some public task.

placebo   A sugar pill that looks like a real medication but doesn't contain any active ingredient.

psychiatrist   A medical doctor who specializes in the diagnosis and treatment of mental illnesses and emotional problems.

psychologist   A mental health professional who provides assessment and treatment for mental and emotional disorders.

psychotherapy   Therapy that uses psychological and behavioral methods to treat mental and emotional disorders.

reuptake   The process by which a neurotransmitter is absorbed back into the nerve cell that originally released it.

Section 504   A section of the Rehabilitation Act of 1973 that applies to students who have a physical or mental impairment that substantially limits one or more major life activities.

selective serotonin reuptake inhibitor (SSRI)   An antidepressant that increases the concentration and activity of serotonin in the brain. SSRIs are widely prescribed for anxiety disorders as well as depression.

serotonin   A neurotransmitter that helps regulate mood, sleep, appetite, and sexual drive.

serotonin-norepinephrine reuptake inhibitor (SNRI)   An antidepressant that affects the concentration and activity of serotonin and norepinephrine in the brain. SNRIs are sometimes prescribed for anxiety disorders as well as depression.

serotonin syndrome   An adverse drug reaction in which there is too much serotonin in the brain.

shyness   A general tendency to pull back from social situations.

social anxiety disorder   An anxiety disorder characterized by marked fear in social situations that involve being around unfamiliar people or the possibility of scrutiny by others.

social phobia   See social anxiety disorder.

specific phobia   An anxiety disorder characterized by intense fear that is focused on a particular animal, object, or situation and that is out of proportion to any real threat.

State Child Health Insurance Program (SCHIP)   A government program that provides health insurance for the children in certain lower-income families who aren't eligible for Medicaid.

support group   A group of people with a common problem who get together to share emotional support and practical advice.

synapse   The tiny space between nerve cells in the brain and body.

temperament   Genetically based personality traits that first show up early in life and tend to stay relatively stable for a long time.

virtual reality exposure therapy   A therapeutic technique that delivers imagery and sound through a special helmet to create the illusion of actually being inside a computer-generated scene. This allows people to simulate exposure to a feared situation.

Resources

Organizations

All of these organizations provide information about some aspect of social anxiety disorder or mental illness. Those marked with an asterisk (*) also offer a toll-free phone number or searchable online directory for locating mental health care providers.

Active Minds on Campus
1875 Connecticut Ave. NW, Suite 418
Washington, DC 20009
(202) 719-1177
www.activemindsoncampus.org

*American Academy of Child and Adolescent Psychiatry
3615 Wisconsin Ave. NW
Washington, DC 20016
(202) 966-7300
www.aacap.org
www.parentsmedguide.org

*American Psychiatric Association
1000 Wilson Blvd., Suite 1825
Arlington, VA 22209
(888) 357-7924
www.psych.org
www.healthyminds.org
www.parentsmedguide.org

*American Psychological Association
750 First St. NE
Washington, DC 20002
(800) 374-2721
www.apa.org
www.apahelpcenter.org
www.psychologymatters.org

*Anxiety Disorders Association of America
8730 Georgia Ave., Suite 600
Silver Spring, MD 20910
(240) 485-1001
www.adaa.org
www.gotanxiety.org

*Association for Behavioral and Cognitive Therapies
305 Seventh Ave., 16th Floor
New York, NY 10001
(212) 647-1890
www.abct.org

Bazelon Center for Mental Health Law
1101 15th St. NW, Suite 1212
Washington, DC 20005
(202) 467-5730
www.bazelon.org

Freedom From Fear
308 Seaview Ave.
Staten Island, NY 10305
(718) 351-1717
www.freedomfromfear.org

NARSAD, The National Mental Health Research Association
60 Cutter Mill Rd., Suite 404
Great Neck, NY 11021
(800) 829-8289
www.narsad.org

National Alliance on Mental Illness
Colonial Place Three
2107 Wilson Blvd., Suite 300

Arlington, VA 22201
(800) 950-6264
www.nami.org

*National Association of Social Workers
750 First St. NE, Suite 700
Washington, DC 20002
(202) 408-8600
www.socialworkers.org
www.helpstartshere.org

National Institute of Mental Health
6001 Executive Blvd., Room 8184, MSC 9663
Bethesda, MD 20892
(866) 615-6464
www.nimh.nih.gov

National Mental Health Association
2001 N. Beauregard St., 12th Floor
Alexandria, VA 22311
(800) 969-6642
www.nmha.org

*National Mental Health Information Center
P.O. Box 42557
Washington, DC 20015
(800) 789-2647
www.mentalhealth.samhsa.gov

Parent Advocacy Coalition for Educational Rights
8161 Normandale Blvd.
Minneapolis, MN 55437
(952) 838-9000
www.pacer.org

Toastmasters International
P.O. Box 9052
Mission Viejo, CA 92690
(949) 858-8255
www.toastmasters.org

Books

Antony, Martin M. *10 Simple Solutions to Shyness: How to Overcome Shyness, Social Anxiety and Fear of Public Speaking.* Oakland, CA: New Harbinger, 2004.

Antony, Martin M., and Richard P. Swinson. *The Shyness and Social Anxiety Workbook.* Oakland, CA: New Harbinger, 2000.

Heimberg, Richard G., Michael R. Liebowitz, Debra A. Hope, and Franklin R. Schneier (Eds.). *Social Phobia: Diagnosis, Assessment, and Treatment.* New York: Guilford Press, 1995.

Hilliard, Erika B. *Living Fully With Shyness and Social Anxiety: A Comprehensive Guide to Gaining Social Confidence.* New York: Marlowe and Company, 2005.

Markway, Barbara G., and Gregory P. Markway. *Painfully Shy: How to Overcome Social Anxiety and Reclaim Your Life.* New York: St. Martin's Griffin, 2001.

Ross, Jerilyn. *Triumph Over Fear: A Book of Help and Hope for People With Anxiety, Panic Attacks, and Phobias.* New York: Bantam, 1994.

Stein, Murray B., and John R. Walker. *Triumph Over Shyness: Conquering Shyness and Social Anxiety.* New York: McGraw-Hill, 2002.

First-Person Accounts

Blyth, Jamie, with Jenna Glatzer. *Fear Is No Longer My Reality: How I Overcame Panic and Social Anxiety Disorder—And You Can Too.* New York: McGraw-Hill, 2005.

Web Sites

Medical Research Network, www.medicalresearchnetwork.com

MindZone, Annenberg Foundation Trust at Sunnylands with the Annenberg Public Policy Center of the University of Pennsylvania, www.CopeCareDeal.org

Social Anxiety Research Clinic, Columbia University/New York Psychiatric Institute, www.columbia-socialanxiety.org

TeensHealth, Nemours Foundation, www.teenshealth.org

Help for Related Problems

Depression

ORGANIZATIONS

Depression and Bipolar Support Alliance, (800) 826-3632, www.dbsalliance.org

Depression and Related Affective Disorders Association, (410) 583-2919, www.drada.org

Families for Depression Awareness, (781) 890-0220, www.familyaware.org

BOOKS

Irwin, Cait, with Dwight L. Evans and Linda Wasmer Andrews. *Monochrome Days: A Firsthand Account of One Teenager's Experience With Depression.* New York: Oxford University Press with the Annenberg Foundation Trust at Sunnylands and the Annenberg Public Policy Center at the University of Pennsylvania, 2007.

Eating Disorders

ORGANIZATIONS

Academy for Eating Disorders, (847) 498-4274, www.aedweb.org

National Association of Anorexia Nervosa and Associated Disorders, (847) 831-3438, www.anad.org

National Eating Disorders Association, (800) 931-2237 www.nationaleatingdisorders.org

BOOKS

Arnold, Carrie, with B. Timothy Walsh. *Next to Nothing: A Firsthand Account of One Teenager's Experience With an Eating Disorder.* New York: Oxford University Press with the Annenberg Foundation Trust at Sunnylands and the Annenberg Public Policy Center at the University of Pennsylvania, 2007.

WEB SITES

Anorexia Nervosa and Related Eating Disorders, www.anred.com

Substance Abuse

ORGANIZATIONS

Alcoholics Anonymous, (212) 870-3400 (check your phone book for a local number), www.aa.org

American Council for Drug Education, (800) 488-3784, www.acde.org

Narcotics Anonymous, (818) 773-9999, www.na.org

National Council on Alcoholism and Drug Dependence, (800) 622-2255, www.ncadd.org

National Institute on Alcohol Abuse and Alcoholism, (301) 443–3860, www.niaaa.nih.gov, and www.collegedrinkingprevention.gov

National Institute on Drug Abuse, (301) 443-1124, www.drugabuse.gov, www.teens.drugabuse.gov

Partnership for a Drug-Free America, (212) 922-1560, www.drugfreeamerica.com

Substance Abuse and Mental Health Services Administration, (800) 729-6686, www.ncadi.samhsa.gov, www.csat.samhsa.gov, www.prevention.samhsa.gov

BOOKS

Keegan, Kyle, with Howard B. Moss, M.D., and Beryl Lieff Benderly. *Chasing the High: A Firsthand Account of One Young Person's Experience with Substance Abuse.* New York: Oxford University Press with the Annenberg Foundation Trust at Sunnylands and the Annenberg Public Policy Center at the University of Pennsylvania, forthcoming in 2008.

WEB SITES

Facts on Tap, Phoenix House, www.factsontap.org

Freevibe, National Youth Anti-Drug Media Campaign, www.freevibe.com

The New Science of Addiction: Genetics and the Brain, Genetic Science Learning Center at the University of Utah, www.gslc.genetics.utah.edu/units/addiction

Suicidal thoughts

ORGANIZATIONS

American Foundation for Suicide Prevention, (888) 333-2377, www.afsp.org

Jed Foundation, (212) 647-7544, www.jedfoundation.org

Suicide Awareness Voices of Education, (952) 946-7998, www.save.org

Suicide Prevention Action Network USA, (202) 449-3600, www.spanusa.org

HOTLINES

National Hopeline Network, (800) 784-2433, www.hopeline.com

National Suicide Prevention Lifeline, (800) 273-8255, www.suicideprevention lifeline.org

BOOKS

Lezine, DeQuincy A., Ph.D., with David Brent, M.D. *Eight Stories Up: An Adolescent Chooses Hope Over Suicide.* New York: Oxford University Press with the Annenberg Foundation Trust at Sunnylands and the Annenberg Public Policy Center at the University of Pennsylvania, forthcoming in 2008.

Bibliography

Books

American Psychiatric Association. *Diagnostic and Statistical Manual of Mental Disorders* (4th ed., text revision). Washington, DC: American Psychiatric Association, 2000.

Evans, Dwight L., Edna B. Foa, Raquel E. Gur, Herbert Hendin, Charles P. O'Brien, Martin E. P. Seligman, and B. Timothy Walsh (Eds.). *Treating and Preventing Adolescent Mental Health Disorders: What We Know and What We Don't Know.* New York: Oxford University Press with the Annenberg Foundation Trust at Sunnylands and the Annenberg Public Policy Center of the University of Pennsylvania, 2005.

Foa, Edna B., and Linda Wasmer Andrews. *If Your Adolescent Has an Anxiety Disorder: An Essential Resource for Parents.* New York: Oxford University Press with the Annenberg Foundation Trust at Sunnylands and the Annenberg Public Policy Center at the University of Pennsylvania, 2006.

Heimberg, Richard G., Michael R. Liebowitz, Debra A. Hope, and Franklin R. Schneier (Eds.). *Social Phobia: Diagnosis, Assessment, and Treatment.* New York: Guilford Press, 1995.

Hope, Debra A., Richard G. Heimberg, and Cynthia L. Turk. *Managing Social Anxiety: A Cognitive-Behavioral Therapy Approach—Therapist Guide.* New York: Oxford University Press, 2006.

Kearney, Christopher A. *Social Anxiety and Social Phobia in Youth: Characteristics, Assessment, and Psychological Treatment.* New York: Springer, 2005.

Merrell, Kenneth W. *Helping Students Overcome Depression and Anxiety: A Practical Guide.* New York: Guilford Press, 2001.

Morris, Tracy L., and John S. March (Eds.). *Anxiety Disorders in Children and Adolescents* (2nd ed.). New York: Guilford Press, 2004.

Ollendick, Thomas H., and John S. March. *Phobic and Anxiety Disorders in Children and Adolescents: A Clinician's Guide to Effective Psychosocial and Pharmacological Interventions.* New York: Oxford University Press, 2004.

Journal Articles

Beidel, Deborah C., Samuel M. Turner, and Tracy L. Morris. Psychopathology of childhood social phobia. *Journal of the American Academy of Child and Adolescent Psychiatry* 38 (1999): 643–650.

Heinrichs, Nina, Ronald M. Rapee, Lynn A. Alden, Susan Bögels, Stefan G. Hofmann, Kyung Ja Oh, and Yuji Sakano. Cultural differences in perceived social norms and social anxiety. *Behaviour Research and Therapy* 44 (2006): 1187–1197.

Hofmann, Stefan G., Alicia E. Meuret, Jasper A. J. Smits, Naomi M. Simon, Mark H. Pollack, Katherine Eisenmenger, Michael Shiekh, and Michael W. Otto. Augmentation of exposure therapy with D-cycloserine for social anxiety disorder. *Archives of General Psychiatry* 63 (2006): 298–304.

Kaye, Walter H., Cynthia M. Bulik, Laura Thornton, Nicole Barbarich, Kim Masters, and the Price Foundation Collaborative Group. Comorbidity of anxiety disorders with anorexia and bulimia nervosa. *American Journal of Psychiatry* 161 (2004): 2215–2221.

Liebowitz, M. R., J. M. Gorman, A. J. Fyer, and D. F. Klein. Social phobia: Review of a neglected anxiety disorder. *Archives of General Psychiatry* 42 (1985): 729–736.

Reports

American College Health Association. *American College Health Association-National College Health Assessment.* Baltimore, MD: American College Health Association, April 2006.

Index

Note: SAD refers to social anxiety disorder. Page numbers followed by "*t*" refer to text boxes and tables.

147